The Marling Menu-Master for France

The Marling Menu-Master for Italy

The Marling Menu-Master for Spain

The

Marling

Menu – Master

for

GERMANY

A comprehensive manual
for translating the German menu
into American English

By

WILLIAM E. and CLARE F. MARLING

ALTARINDA BOOKS
13 Estates Drive
Orinda, CA 94563

TABLE OF CONTENTS

PRICES LISTED ON PRACTICE MENU ARE NOT ACTUAL ONES.

INTRODUCTION

Your trip to Germany is part of a grand adventure!

It is not necessary to frequent only the grand deluxe restaurants and hotels where the serving of Continental foods is much the same as everywhere in Europe, and where the maitre d'hotel and waiters all speak adequate English. But, rather try the myriad other German restaurants, upper middle class, the middle, the lower middle, the BIERSTUBE and WEINSTUBE (much like English pubs), where little or no English is spoken, and where truly German food is served.

One of the best ways to get the feel of a country, and to sense being on the inside looking out, rather than on the outside looking in, is to be seated in a restaurant surrounded by the local people all eating their dishes in their fashion.

In Germany the tap water is absolutely safe to drink, the food is carefully and hygienically handled, restaurants and kitchens extremely clean (German law even requires noting on menus any use of artificial sweeteners, preservatives, or coloration).

It is hoped that this book will arm you with confidence, and that it will do much in enabling you quickly to fathom, and to untangle the seeming complexities and strangeness of the German menu.

FOOD SERVING ESTABLISHMENTS

These come under a variety of names, and are listed below roughly according to the variety and amount of cooking and food which they serve, the restaurants being the most complete, but this is only approximate, for a Bierstube run by a brewery can have a colossally vast menu:

RESTAURANT: Complete food and drinks.

RATSKELLER: These are excellent for regional specialties and traditional German food. Each city, town, and village has its RATHAUS, which is its city hall. Except for villages, and very few towns, the Rathaus has its RATSKELLER, which is a restaurant in the cellar of the Rathaus. There are no "Ratskellers" (as found in the United States) as restaurants, other than the genuine one. The Ratskellers are upper medium quality to high quality restaurants, although usually not very expensive, and except where knocked or bombed out in the war, and rebuilt, they are usually in a very historic, old building, dating back to 1360, 1475, 1520 A.D.

GASTSTÄTTE: Is simply the German word for the French word restaurant. In railway stations they are called BAHNHOFSGASTSTÄTTE. They serve complete meals.

GASTHOF: The village, or open country word for restaurant. They serve drinks, and modest to complete meals.

GASTHAUS: The same as Gasthof–a restaurant of more or less modest proportions.

IMBISS: Means snack. A sort of liner-diner, or hot dog stand.

RASTSTÄTTE or RASTHAUS: These are restaurants and restaurant-inns along the AUTOBAHNS (freeways).

BIERSTUBE: Beer parlors much like an English pub, serving drinks and light food.

WEINSTUBE: Wine parlors much like an English pub, serving drinks and light food.

SCHNELLBUFFET: Short-order to cafeteria eateries.

SCHNELLGASTSTÄTTE: Meaning "fast restaurant"; is a short-order house.

SCHNELLIMBISS: Fast snacks, as grilled sausages or hot dogs.

INFORMATION ON SERVINGS

Most hotels of all categories (meaning of all classes and price ranges), except those marked "GARNI" (no restaurant) serve food, and even these hotels have a little breakfast room where the FRÜHSTÜCK (breakfast) is served.

Except for the extremely chic and elaborate, and relatively costly restaurants and hotels, most restaurants are informal in atmosphere, and you find, especially in summer, all combinations of dress.

Due to their custom of serving from abundant to vast quantities of food for each dish, you are not required or expected to order (nor do the Germans) a complete meal in the sense of several dishes, for you could not eat that much.

Care should be exercised in ordering, for it is difficult to eat an appetizer AND a main dish, so much is frequently served on the former. And the more expensive the dish means the more that comes with it, and the more elaborately and abundantly it is garnished.

6

It is not infrequent that you will see in a good restaurant, Germans ordering a glass of beer only, and perhaps an appetizer or a cold plate to go with it. Further, you may enter at nearly any time of the day to have food and drink, although the general eating hours are indicated below. All restaurants serve snacks and open-faced sandwiches (BELEGTES BROT), and appetizers (VORSPEISEN).

The main dish is very similar to our own, in that it comes usually complete with meat, potatoes (and frequently with sauerkraut), cooked vegetables, condiments, and salad. These accompanying items are indicated on the menu, after, but on the same line as the meat, by the word MIT (with).

COCKTAILS

There is no cocktail hour, nor separate bar, except in establishments catering to the international trade. Cocktails are not served, nor hard liquor drunk, except along with a glass of beer, or after a meal. This hard liquor is a SCHNAPS (a liquor distilled from some grain), or BRANNTWEIN (a brandy distilled from some fruit), and is served in a little glass of less than an ounce.

In addition there is a variety of different SPIRITUOSEN (spirits and liqueurs), many with herbal flavor as JÄGERMEISTER or STEINHÄGER, and others of fruit flavor as KIRSCHWASSER, HIMBEERGEIST, ZWETSCHGENWASSER (cherry, raspberry, plum).

Two special beverages of the Main area are hard cider (APFELWEIN), and apple juice (APFELSAFT). A refreshing summer drink is BERLINER WEISSE mit SCHUSS, a light wheat beer with a dash of raspberry juice.

In many places you could order a whisky, or brandy, or cognac, and a glass of water or soda water, and pour your drink into it. Ice may be hard to come by. Colas, other soft drinks, and fruit juices (SAFT) which are canned, abound, and these may be easily ordered.

All of these drinks, both alcoholic and non-alcoholic will be listed on the menu under GETRÄNKE (drinks).

EATING HOURS

BREAKFAST (FRÜHSTÜCK): 7–10 A.M. The Germans rise early, and breakfast consists of some bread, rolls, jam, butter, and coffee (or tea), but you may order additional items such as eggs (normally soft-boiled), cold sausage, cheese. Fresh fruit juice is not available; canned may be had. Frequently, in the medium to smaller hotels the price of the hotel room includes the above simple breakfast, and each hotel, no matter how small, has its FRÜHSTÜCKSZIMMER (breakfast room).

LUNCH (MITTAGESSEN): 12–2 P.M. This can hardly be called lunch, for it is the main meal of the day for most Germans, and they eat heavily at that time. In fact, the daily menu is frequently called the MITTAGSKARTE (mid-day list), instead of TAGESKARTE (daily list). It happens that at night they can be out of certain items which appeared on the daily menu, and sometimes they have an ABENDKARTE (evening list), which is much more restricted in offerings than what is found on the noon list.

DINNER (ABENDESSEN): 6:30–9 P.M. However, many restaurants stay open until 11 P.M., so actually dinner may be had very late if you wish. The Germans generally eat their evening meal early, starting about 6 P.M.

There are, in addition, two more eating times for the Germans, one about 10 A.M., when they have their ZWEITES FRÜHSTÜCK (second breakfast), consisting of bread and sausage with beer, or a pastry with coffee, and then again at about 3–4 P.M. when they have KAFFEE (coffee) with pastries, open-faced pies, cakes with rich frostings and whipped cream, and even whipped cream as a separate dish, ice creams and sundaes, or may even have some cold cuts, cheese or other snacks.

TIPPING

German law now requires that all restaurants and drinking establishments include all taxes and the service charge in the price of each item on the menu or bill of fare. Thus, the price listed for any dish, meal, course, or drink is all inclusive with tax and service already included. This is called ENDPREIS. You will not have any "service" percentage added at the end of your bill.

It is desired and customary, however, to leave an additional small amount of about 5%, especially if the service has been good, and most certainly this is expected in the higher class restaurants and hotels. In the smaller to medium class restaurants, and the Weinstuben and Bierstuben you normally leave the change to round out to an even 50 pfennigs. Watch what the Germans do.

Various seemingly mysterious expressions or sentences are written on the menus to indicate that tax and service are inclusive in your bill, but you do not have to worry about them, for the law which applies to them is general throughout Germany.

THE GERMAN RESTAURANT

Nearly all restaurants and hotels post outside, in the window, or in the foyer or vestibule, in clear view, a copy of their SPEISEKARTE (permanent printed menu), or their TAGESKARTE (daily menu), or both.

Thus, you may examine the menu, decipher what is offered, all without the embarrassment of having a waiter stand by while you painfully, slowly at first, translate individual items. Then, when you enter the restaurant you will have time at the table to check or re-do your examination of the various dishes, this time quicker, and with more assurance.

Usually, when you enter, the waiters will be busy, and you are expected to seek out your own table of your choice. Even where there is a maitre d'hotel, frequently he is also busy, and you are expected to take your own table.

To avoid the awkwardness of standing around with one foot on the other waiting to be seated, it is better to cast a quick glance around, and if nothing indicates that you will be seated, then just walk over and take a table. A waiter will come by soon and leave a menu, and it will be some minutes before he returns to take your order.

Do not be surprised if someone joins you at your table, for this is also the custom, namely, to take a seat wherever one is vacant. This happens in the smaller restaurants.

BEVERAGES SERVED WITH MEALS

BEER (BIER): Is drunk with the meals. You will note by looking around that nearly everyone has a glass of beer, either on tap (vom FASS) or from a bottle (FLASCHE), for it is the national drink, and is not especially considered an alcoholic beverage as it is in America. It is their beverage, simply that.

WINE (WEIN): Both white (WEISS) and red (ROT), is offered by the glass (SCHOPPEN), as well as by the bottle, for due to high taxes, wine by the bottle is relatively expensive by German standards. The purchase by the glass is an excellent way of tasting various of the wonderful white German Rhine, Mosel, Rheingau and other wines.

COFFEE (KAFFEE): Is not drunk or served with the meal, for coffee, due to the high taxes, is very costly, and when you do have a cup after a meal, it is a small cup (costing about 30 cents) and stronger than our coffee, but not as strong as in France or Italy.

WATER (WASSER): Is not served at the table, and will not be brought to you unless you ask for it, and then you may have to follow it up with another reminder to bring it.

OTHER BEVERAGES: Milk (MILCH), tea (TEE), canned fruit juice (SAFT), soft drinks and colas may also be ordered with meals.

All beverages, both alcoholic and non-alcoholic are listed on the back of the menu under GETRÄNKE (Drinks)

Bread (BROT) or rolls (BRÖTCHEN), are not served with meals, unless the specific dish indicates that they come with that dish, but bread and rolls may be had for the asking, and will be charged extra on your bill.

THE MENU

The general, permanent printed menu (SPEISEKARTE is broken down into as many as sixteen food categories cold pre-courses, hot pre-courses, soups, beef meat pork meat, veal meat, etc. Whereas the daily menu (TAGESKARTE), after listing any fixed price meal (GEDECK), and the soups, is usually a conglomerate of dishes, listed one right after the other in a bewildering closely lined, typed, seeming jumble of dishes with their garnishes.

On this Tageskarte you will find about the only fixed price meals (GEDECK) offered, price varying with the entree (meat), and the elaborateness of the accompanying garnishes. Soup, which is a great favorite with the Germans, will always be one of the fixed price meal dishes, and in addition to the meat, a modest dessert is usually also included.

Further soups will be offered on the upper part of the Tageskarte just before where the main dishes a la carte are listed. The fish, meats, fowl, and wild game will all be interspersed in this general listing on the Tageskarte.

Following are the different Speisekarte categories with translations. Not all will be encountered on any one menu, and some different expressions or spellings for the same category will crop up; contrived, or invented expressions for these same categories have not been included.

BREAKDOWN OF THE MENU

(By categories in order encountered, including various expressions for the same category)

BELEGTES BROT: Open-faced sandwiches.

KALTE GERICHTE: Small to medium sized cold plates.

KALTE VORGERICHTE: Cold first courses or appetizers.

KALTE VORSPEISEN: Same as above.

KLEINE GERICHTE: Small courses, hot or cold.

SCHNITTEN: Plate of snacks, cold cuts, and vegetables.

WARME GERICHTE: Hot small to medium sized (in quantity) dishes.

TELLERGERICHTE: Plate courses, hot or cold.

WARME VORGERICHTE: Hot first courses or appetizers.

VORSPEISEN: First courses, or appetizers.

WURST-SPEZIALITÄTEN: House specialties in hot sausages.

WURSTGERICHTE: Sausage dishes, usually hot.

SUPPEN: Soup dishes.

EIERSPEISEN und MEHLSPEISEN: Egg dishes, and flour-made dishes, as noodles, dumplings, spaghetti.

MEHLSPEISEN: Flour-made dishes, as noodles, dumplings, omelette-pancakes, and can also mean sweet desserts made of flour.

PFANNENGERICHTE: Omelette-like, pan-fried pancakes, wide diameter.

TEIGWAREN: Flour-made dishes as spaghetti, noodles, dumplings.

11

FISCH: Fish dishes.
FISCHGERICHTE: Fish dishes.

GEFLÜGEL: Fowl, both domestic and wild.
GEFLÜGEL und WILD: Fowl, domestic and wild, and wild game dishes.
WILD: Wild game dishes (deer, wild pig, etc.).

HAUPTGERICHTE: Main courses or dishes; main courses as opposed to first courses, or small dishes, or appetizers.
FERTIGE SPEISEN: Ready cooked, or ready to serve main dishes.
FLEISCHGERICHTE: Meat dishes.
GRILLGERICHTE: Dishes from the grill.
KALTE SPEISEN: Cold main dishes.
SPEZIALITÄTEN: Specialties of the house.
WARME SPEISEN: Hot main dishes.
VOM GRILL: Dishes from the grill.
VOM HAMMEL: Mutton main dishes.
VOM LAMM: Lamb main dishes.
VOM KALB: Veal main dishes.
VOM RIND: Beef main dishes.
VOM ROST: Main dishes, grilled, roasted, or broiled.
VOM SCHWEIN: Pork main dishes.
VOM SPIESS: Skewered dishes, can be from spit, or braised.

BEILAGEN: Supplemental dishes, vegetables, salads, starches.
GEMÜSE und BEILAGEN: Vegetables and other supplemental dishes.
GEMÜSE: Vegetables.
GEMÜSE und SALATE: Vegetables and salads (not the ones with mayonnaise).

KÄSE: Various cheeses offered.

EIS: Ice creams.
EISSPEZIALITÄTEN: Ice cream specialties.
KOMPOTTE: Cooked or stewed fruits, fresh or dried.
NACHSPEISEN: Desserts, sweet dishes.
NACHTISCH: Desserts, sweet dishes.
SÜSS-SPEISEN: Desserts, sweet dishes.

ATTACKING THE MENU

Most of the items in the first few categories are more or less straight forward on the menu, but when you face the main courses, meat, fish or fowl—the confusion starts.

Just as we do, so do the Germans describe dishes as fresh, mouth-watering, succulent, deep-sea, or farm cottage smoked; but the Germans, in their language can tack these descriptive words on either the front end or the rear end of the main word, stringing them all together in a confusing chain of letters, and thus burying the key word—WHAT IS IT? To discover what it is you must learn to recognize the principal listings in the meat, fish and fowl categories, find them in the translation, and then work backwards or forward from there.

For example, in the meat section you will have to learn KALB, veal; RIND, beef; SCHWEIN, pork; HAMMEL, mutton; LAMM, lamb; SCHINKEN, ham; OCHSEN, ox or steer; REH, roebuck; HIRSCH, a large deer. In the fowl section you will have to learn HUHN or GEFLÜGEL, chicken; ENTE, duck; GANS, goose, and in the fish section FORELLE, trout; SEEZUNGE, sole; HEILBUTT, halibut; HERING, herring.

When you have learned to recognize these few important words, the menu quickly starts to untangle then, for if it is KALB (veal), next will come what part of the animal as KEULE (leg). Then comes the method of preparation, as GEBRATEN (roasted, braised) or what not. Ahead of the word Kalb may be attached a description of its being fattened, and perhaps where it is from, as in SCHLESWIGER MAST**KALBS**KEULE GEBRATEN. Honestly, this happens on menus, even though by correct German orthography it should be separated into three distinct words. It means roasted leg of fattened veal from the Schleswig region. Our endeavor is to list these dishes in such a fashion that with the key word the translating is quick and easy.

"ART"
(Style)

Then, on the same line will be how it is prepared, if not simply roasted or braised, as in the veal dish mentioned above, it will be followed by the use of the word "ART", which the Germans use to mean "after the style of", or "in the fashion of", or "how so-and-so does it", as in "JÄGER ART", "HAUSFRAUEN ART", "MÜLLERIN ART"— hunter style, housewife style, miller's wife's style, or simply "JÄGER", or "ROSSINI", or "WESTMORELAND". Of the more than 100 preparations of this nature we have listed only those most frequently encountered.

You will often encounter the word "WIENER" on menus. It means Vienna (WIEN) in Austria—as in Wienerschnitzel, Kalbschnitzel "Wiener Art", or simply Schnitzel "Wiener Art". All mean the same breaded veal cutlet which is the manner of preparing this cut of meat in Vienna. The use of the word "HAMBURGER" means how it is done in Hamburg. If you are looking for our hamburger, it is called "DEUTSCHES BEEFSTEAK". "BAYERISCH" means Bavarian, and "FRANKFURTER" means from Frankfort or Frankfort style.

MIT
(With)

After this comes the "MIT", or what is served with this meat dish as a garnish or accompaniment, as some preparation of potatoes, or sauerkraut, or cooked vegetables, and condiments, cooked fruit, sauces, or ALL of these things, and possibly on one plate!

A WORD ABOUT THE MEAT

As it is with ours, so it is with German meals that the meat is THE thing. A sketchy and partial explanation of how they cut their meat, what parts are used, mention of certain complexities in words used for the cooking, and the reminding of the world-wide known vagaries of the chef's work, should do much toward easing further the unravelling of the menu.

The Germans cut their beef and other animals very differently from the way Americans do, and usually bone out the meat. Where possible they cut along the tendons and natural separations, whereas we cut across the meat.

The result is that the name for one cut of their meat can include several cuts of ours. For instance, what they call roastbeef (RINDERRÜCKEN) is boneless, and encompasses all the loin from the ribsteaks on back including the club, T-bone, porterhouse, and even a portion of the top sirloin.

So, in ordering a piece of roastbeef it is impossible to know whether you will receive a piece of rib steak, or a piece of porterhouse (minus the tenderloin).

In translating the dishes, a careful effort has been made to translate each German cut accurately into the closest equivalent, or actual American cut of meat.

A further complication is that some cuts of meat are called by how they are usually cooked rather than by the part of the animal from which they come, such as ROSTBRATEN, literally meaning roasted in the oven on a grilled frame (ROST), but this is a cut of beef or veal from our prime rib area, and is called ROSTBRATEN on the menu, or in the butcher shop.

ATTENTION

All parts of the animals are used in Germany, nothing is wasted–the ears, lungs, jowls, stomach, face, tail, feet, udders, in addition to the tongue, heart, liver, kidneys, and sweetbreads. So, in order to avoid any surprises when your dish arrives at the table, it will pay you to acquaint yourself with these meat parts, or check them in the meat dishes list when ordering. Also, by doing this you will not miss, or deprive yourself of the pleasure of tasting the many and varied, exceptionally excellent and fine-tasting German main dishes.

COOKING TERMS

There is no separate word in German used actually to distinguish clearly among roasted, fried, baked, grilled, broiled. GEBRATEN can mean all of these (and on occasion so can GEBACKEN), and is constantly used on menus. It can even mean braised!

Certain meats and fishes are normally fried, certain others are broiled, others are braised, others are baked, and when they are listed on the menu as GEBRATEN (or GEBACKEN), it frequently means done in their normal German fashion of cooking.

They either are not concerned with, or already know what happens, but we don't. So, these multiple uses of the words Gebraten and Gebacken have been resolved on the fish-dish, and on the meat-dish lists in American terminology, so that you will know how your selection is to be cooked, or how it should be cooked. In this way you will not receive something dunked in a batter and deep-fried when you expected it to be grilled.

Finally, before you launch into your quest for finding out "What it is", we remind you that as everywhere, chefs are "Artistes", and even giving a dish the same name as the original French, or Hungarian, or Italian one, the chef is likely to apply German overtones to it; and for his German dishes, either lacking certain ingredients, or partial to others, or on his own inspiration, he further applies a twist.

For these reasons, some constantly encountered dishes on the menus will not be prepared exactly the same way in each restaurant. For example, a Schnitzel "Jäger Art", can vary from place to place as to taste of the sauce, and the garnish accompanying the dish.

ABBREVIATIONS

Be prepared for many abbreviations on the menus. The length of the words, and the lack of space for writing them brings about odd abbreviations. We list some of the common ones; but usually if you check under the first two letters or so you will find the word alphabetically listed in the translation.

PRACTICE MENU

At the back of your Menu-Master is a fold-out reproduction of a typical German daily menu, a TAGES-KARTE, The list would be changed to a certain degree each day. To gain some experience before facing your first meal in Germany, we suggest that you decipher, with the aid of your book, the offerings listed on this menu.

VORSPEISEN
(Appetizers, First Courses)

These are appetizers, snacks, sandwiches, first courses or light meals. They may be listed on the menus under any of the following names, and will be found translated in this section.

BELEGTES BROT: Open faced sandwiches.

KALTE GERICHTE: Small to medium sized cold plates.

KLEINE GERICHTE: Small courses, hot or cold.

KALTE VORGERICHTE: Cold first courses or appetizers.

TELLERGERICHTE: Plate courses, as mixed cold cuts.

WARME GERICHTE: Hot small to medium sized dishes.

WARME VORGERICHTE: Hot first courses or hot appetizers.

SCHNITTEN: Plate of snacks, cold cuts and vegetables.

KALTE VORSPEISEN: Cold first courses or appetizers.

WARME VORSPEISEN: Warm or hot first courses or appetizers.

VORSPEISEN: First courses or appetizers.

WURSTGERICHTE: Sausage dishes, usually hot.

WURST-SPEZIALITÄTEN: House specialties in hot sausages. (Sausages are listed in a separate category in this section under WÜRSTE)

EIERSPEISEN und MEHLSPEISEN
(Egg and Flour-made Dishes)

These are the egg dishes, and the starch dishes, as noodles, dumplings, omelette-pancakes, and will be found variously listed as follows:

EIERSPEISEN: Egg dishes.

MEHLSPEISEN: Starch dishes (flour-made products) and also sweet desserts made of flour.

PFANNENGERICHTE: Omelette-like, pan-fried, wide diameter pancakes.

TEIGWAREN: Flour-made dishes such as spaghetti, noodles, macaroni.

VORSPEISEN
(Appetizers, First Courses)

Both WARME (warm or hot) and KALTE (cold) VOR-
SPEISEN (appetizers) are offered as a first course in a full
meal, or as a light meal in themselves, but they are
much more hearty dishes that what we know as appetizers,
the mixture of delicate concoctions usually served with
drinks during the cocktail hour. Contrary to the custom in
Latin countries of eating small quantities of mixed
appetizers for a first course, the Germans prefer to order
only one appetizer and therefore expect it to be a generous
portion.

As cold appetizers you will find herring, a German
favorite, served in many different ways, smoked salmon,
trout or eel; caviar, sardines, anchovies; seafood cocktails;
raw or cooked ham; a variety of salads made of herring
chicken, cold meats and sausages, tuna, seafood
vegetables, mostly served with a rich, thick mayonnaise.

Warm appetizers are usually served AUF TOAST (on
toast) and cold ones with different types of BROT (bread)
or BRÖTCHEN (rolls) and BUTTER (butter). They may also
come with some kind of KARTOFFELN (potatoes)
perhaps a GEMÜSE (vegetable) or some garnish including
FRUCHT (fruit), which will also be indicated in the
listing on the menu.

BELEGTES BROT is the German version of the sandwich, always open-faced and eaten with a knife and fork.
Ingredients served on many different types of bread o
rolls include ham, all types of cold roast meats, sausages
anchovies, herring, salmon, sardines, cheese. A smoked
salmon sandwich for example, may be listed as BROT mi
LACHS (bread with salmon) or LACHSBROT (salmon
bread).

Frequently restaurants or cafes list a GEMISCHTE KALTE
VORSPEISEN, a mixed plate of various cold cuts, cheese
cold chicken, with such garnishes as pickles, tomatoes
radishes, olives and hard-boiled eggs. An appetizer o
this size is really a meal in itself.

Aside from the vast variety of WÜRSTE (sausages) which
are listed separately in this section, probably the mos
popular warm appetizer in Germany is the KÖNIGIN
PASTETE or "Queen's Pastry"—a patty shell filled with
diced chicken in a thick, rich, cream sauce referred to a
RAGOUT' This dish is a version of our "Chicken a la King"

AAL: Eel.

ANANAS: Pineapple.

APFEL: Apple.

AUFSCHNITT: Cold cuts.

AUF: On, as in Auf Toast—on toast.

AUSTERN: Oysters.

BACHKREBS: Stream crayfish.

BAUERN-: Farm-style.

    Frühstück: Peasant breakfast—boiled potatoes fried, mixed with scrambled eggs and pieces of ham, garnished with pickles.

    Geräuchertes: Farm-cured smoked meats.

    Hinterschinken: Farm-style cured ham.

    Hoppel-Poppel: Peasant breakfast with veal meat instead of ham or bacon.

BEEFSTEAK TARTAR: Raw ground beef with raw egg mixed in, and garnished with chopped capers, anchovies, raw onions and parsley.

BELEGTES BROT: Sandwiches, open-faced, eaten with knife and fork.

BISMARCKHERING: Fresh herring filets pickled in vinegar, mustard seed, peppercorns, sliced raw onions, and spices.

BLÄTTERTEIGPASTETE(CHEN): Patty shell.

    mit **Feinem Kalbsfleischragout:** With diced veal in a rich, brown cream sauce.

    mit **Geflügelragout:** With diced chicken or other fowl in rich cream sauce.

    mit **Krebsschwänzchen:** With crayfish tails in a cream sauce.

BORDELAISE-SAUCE: Made with stock and red wine and flavored with chopped shallots, herbs and with beef marrow added.

BRATEN-: Cold roast meats.

    Platte: A plate of slices of various cold roast meats.

    Sülze: Cold roast meats in aspic.

BROT: Bread. When combined with other words such as LACHSBROT or KÄSEBROT, it means an open-faced sandwich, in this case, of salmon or cheese.

BRÖTCHEN: Rolls.

BROTZEIT-TELLER: Mid-morning plate of meat and other snacks.

BÜNDNERFLEISCH: An air-dried cured beef usually sliced wafer thin.

BUTTER: Butter.

CAVIAR: Caviar (Beluga, Belugastör, Malossol)–the grey, lightly salted roe of the Beluga, largest member of the sturgeon family.

CHAMPIGNONS: Mushrooms, the French word.

à la **Creme:** Mushrooms in a cream sauce.

au **Gratin:** With a sauce and then put under broiler to brown on top.

DILL-SAUCE: A white sauce with chopped dill and other herbs.

DOSE: Can or tin, as of sardines.

ECHTE(R): Genuine.

EDEL: Fine quality.

Fischmayonnaise: Fine quality fried or boiled fish with mayonnaise.

EI(ER)-: Eggs.

Salat: Egg salad with mayonnaise.

EIS: Ice.

EISBEIN in ASPIK: Pork shank, what we call hock, in aspic.

ESSIG: Vinegar.

FEIN(E)(ER): Fine or delicate.

FIN: Same as above.

FISCH-: Fish.

Mayonnaise: Cold boiled fish with mayonnaise.

FLEISCH-: Meat.

Füllung: Meat filling.

Käse: A meat loaf made of beef and other minced meats.

Salat: Meat salad–strips of cooked meat, sausage, chopped pickles, onions with mayonnaise dressing.

Sülze: Meat in aspic.

FLUSSLACHS: Stream salmon.

FORELLENFILET: Filet of trout.

FRANKFURTER: From Frankfort, or Frankfort-style.

FRISCH(E)(ER): Fresh.

FROSCHSCHENKEL: Frog legs.

GANZ(E)(ER): Whole, entire.

GÄNSELEBER-: Goose liver, pure, preserved or a paste of goose liver.

Pastete: Goose liver paté or paste.

GARNIERT(E): Garnished.

GEBACKEN: Fried, can also mean deep-fried.

GEBRATEN: Means roasted principally, but can mean fried or braised, generally means cooked.

GEEISTE MELONE: Chilled melon.

GEFLÜGEL: Chicken.

GEFLÜGEL: (cont.)

    Leber: Chicken livers.

    Leber "Strassburger Art" im Reisrand: Chicken livers cooked in red wine sauce, served with mushrooms on a rice ring.

    Salat: Chicken salad with mayonnaise.

GEFÜLLTE: Stuffed or filled.

GEKOCHT(ER): Cooked, usually means boiled.

GEMISCHT(ER): Mixed.

GEMÜSESALAT: Vegetable salad.

GEPÖKELT: Pickled.

GERÄUCHERT(ER): Smoked.

GERÖSTETE: Roasted.

GESCHABTES TARTARENSTEAK GARNIERT: Finely ground raw beef mixed with raw egg, garnished with chopped raw onions, capers, anchovies and parsley.

GESÜLZTES: In aspic.

GURKE(N): Cucumber.

HAUS-: House or home.

    Gebeizt: Home-cured.

    Gemachte: Homemade.

    Macher: Same as above.

HANDKÄSE mit MUSIK: A strong-flavored cheese from Mainzer or Harzer areas which is sliced in square or medallion form, marinated in a sauce of vinegar, oil, salt and pepper, served with raw minced onions and bread.

HAPPEN: Morsel, snack.

HAWAII: With pineapple garnish.

HERING(S)-: Herring.

    Filet: Filet.

    "Hausfrauenart": Housewife's style– (see Matjeshering).

HOLZBRETT: Wooden plank.

HOLZTELLER: Wooden plate.

HUMMER: Lobster.

HUMMERKRABBEN: Large prawns.

ITALIENISCHER SALAT: Italian salad–should be a salad of mixed diced vegetables garnished with anchovy filets, capers, olives, hard-boiled eggs with mayonnaise dressing, but wide variations exist, can have chopped ham and other ingredients.

KALB(S)-: Veal.

    Braten: Cold cooked veal.

    Käse: A veal meat loaf.

KALT(ER): Cold.

KAPERN: Capers.

KAROTTEN-EINTOPF mit FLEISCHEINLAGE: Carrot casserole with meat added.

KÄSE: Cheese.

KASSELER: Pickled, smoked pork loin chop with bone in.
    Saftrippe: Juicy pickled and smoked pork loin chop.

KATENRAUCHSCHINKEN: Cottage-smoked ham, style of.

KATENRAUCHSPECK in PAPRIKA: Paprika-covered, cottage-smoked bacon, style of.

KAVIAR: Caviar, usually the lightly salted grey roe of the Beluga, largest member of the sturgeon family.

KLEIN aber FEIN: General heading on menus for small, tasty dishes; or a small veal steak on toast with garnish.

KÖNIGIN PASTETE(CHEN): Queen's pastry, a filled patty shell.
    mit **Feinem Ragout Gefüllt(e):** Patty shell filled with diced chicken in a rich, cream sauce with mushrooms, wine, herbs. Our Chicken a la King.

KOPFSALAT: Lettuce salad.

KRABBEN-: Generic term for various shrimp and prawns.
    Mayonnaise: Shrimp in mayonnaise dressing.
    Salat: Shrimp salad with mayonnaise.

KRÄUTER-: Herbs.
    Butter: Herbal butter.
    Quark: Cottage cheese seasoned with chopped herbs.

KREBS-: Freshwater crayfish or crawdads.
    Fleisch: Crayfish meat.
    Schwänze: Crayfish tails.

LACHS or LACHS-SALM: Salmon.

LAND: Country-style, or local, or of the area.

LANGUSTENMAYONNAISE: Sea crayfish (California lobster) with mayonnaise.

LEBER-: Liver.
    Käse: Cold or hot meat loaf made of liver, pork, and bacon, seasoned with herbs.
    Pressack: Pressed meat loaf made of liver.

LUCULLUS-EIER: Can be poached, boiled, scrambled eggs with goose-liver, truffle and other garnishes in different preparations with various sauces.

MARINIERTES: Marinated.

MASTRINDFLEISCH-SALAT: Cold, cooked, grain fed beef cut in strips and put into a salad with mayonnaise.

MATJESHERING: Young herring, which has not yet spawned.

"Hausfrauenart": Housewife's style–skinned filets, garnished with raw apple slices, onion rings, pickles, cherry tomatoes, sauce of chopped onions, apples, cayenne pepper with sour cream.

MAYONNAISESALAT: Pieces of cooked meat or fish, vegetables in mayonnaise dressing.

MEERRETTICH: Horseradish.

MEERESFRÜCHTE(N): Seafood.

MILD(ER): Mild.

MITTELMEER: Mediterranean Sea.

MUSCHEL RAGOUT FIN: Mussels in a thick, cream sauce.

NORWEGISCHE EIER: "Norwegian Eggs"–poached eggs, aspic-covered placed on shrimp salad mixed with chopped anchovy filets.

OCHSEN-: Steer beef.

Mark: Beef marrow.

Maulsalat: Beef snout (pickled), sliced thinly and served in a vinegar sauce with sliced raw onions.

Zunge: Ox tongue.

Zungentaschen: Cold sliced tongue rolls with horse-radish sauce inside.

ODER: Or.

ÖL: Oil.

ÖLSARDINEN (1 dose): Sardines packed in oil (one tin).

PASTETE GEFÜLLT mit FEINEM RAGOUT: Patty shell filled with diced veal parts in a thick cream sauce flavored with mushrooms, wine and herbs.

PASTETE KAPUZINERART: Capucine Monk's style–a delicate meat stew served in a patty shell.

PFIFFERLINGE(N): A type of wild mushroom.

PFIRSICH: Peach.

PIKANTE: Piquant, spicy.

PLATTE: Plate.

PÖKEL: Pickled.

PÖKELZUNGE: Pickled tongue.

PRESSACK: A pork headcheese.

QUARK mit FRÜCHTEN: Cottage cheese with fruit.

RAGOUT FIN: A very frequently served dish of diced veal parts, tongue, brains, in a rich cream sauce containing mushrooms, herbs, white wine, enriched with egg. Served in a patty shell or any individual shell or container.

im **Näpfchen:** The above sprinkled with cheese and

23

RAGOUT FIN:
  Im **Näpfchen:** (cont.)
  breadcrumbs and put under broiler.
RAHM: Cream.
RAHMMEERRETTICH: Horseradish cream sauce.
RÄUCH(ER)-: Smoked.
  Aal: Smoked eel.
  Fleisch: Smoked beef.
  Lachs: Smoked salmon.
RAVIOLI in TOMATENTUNKE: Ravioli in tomato sauce.
REGENSBURGER: A small, coarse grained beef and pork
  sausage.
  in **Essig und Öl:** When served cold is cut into slices
  and dressed with oil and vinegar.
REMOULADE: Mayonnaise sauce with mustard, anchovies,
  capers, gherkins, tarragon, chervil.
RESTAURATIONSBROT: One slice of bread served with
  cold cuts and garnished.
RETTICH mit BUTTER: Radishes with butter.
RIESE(N): Large, king size.
RIND(ER)-: Beef.
  Fleisch: Cold cooked beef.
  Fleischsalat "Teufels Art": Cooked beef cut in strips
  and served with a spicy, vinegar sauce.
  Mark: Beef marrow.
RIPPCHEN, RIPPERL, RIPPENSPEER: Pickled, smoked rib
  loin pork chop.
ROASTBEEF (ROSTBEEF): Roastbeef.
  Röllchen: Cold roast beef roll.
ROH(ER): Raw.
ROHKOST: Raw sliced or grated vegetables served as a
  salad.
RÖLLCHEN: Rolls of thinly sliced cold cooked meat,
  usually stuffed.
ROLLMOPS: Small pieces of salt-cured herring, spread
  with mustard, rolled around a piece of onion and pickle
  and some capers.
ROTER und WEISSER PRESSACK: A light and dark
  pressed meat loaf, a Bavarian headcheese.
RÜHREI: Scrambled eggs.
RUNDSTÜCK WARM: Open-faced sandwich of roast meat
  served with a warm gravy—a hot roast beef or pork
  sandwich.
RUSSISCHE EIER: Russian Eggs—halves of hard-boiled
  eggs, sometimes stuffed, covered with mayonnaise,

RUSSISCHE EIER: (cont.)
sometimes with a bit of caviar or other addition, and often serving as garnish for a salad.

RUSSISCHER GEFLÜGELSALAT: Chicken salad with hard-boiled eggs covered with mayonnaise.

SAFTSCHINKEN: Juicy ham.

SAHNE: Cream.

SAHNEMEERRETTICH: Horseradish cream sauce.

SALAMI: Any salami type cold sausage.

SALAT: Salad.

SALM: Salmon.

SARDELLEN: Anchovies.

SARDINEN: Sardines.

SAUCE: Sauce.

SAUER: Sour.

SAUERGURKE: Pickle.

SCAMPICOCKTAIL: Shrimp or prawn cocktail.

SCHEIBEN: Slices.

SCHINKEN-: Ham.
> **Röllchen:** Rolled up ham slices with or without a filling.

SCHLEMMERSCHNITTE: Gourmet dish of large slice of bread spread with raw ground beef, mixed with raw egg, chopped raw onions, capers, anchovies and garnished with caviar and sliced hard-boiled eggs.

SCHNECKEN-: Snails.
> **Ragout "Provencales":** Snails stewed in a sauce of tomatoes and onions.
> **Spiess mit Champignons, Speck, Knoblauch Butter:** Snails cooked on a skewer with mushrooms, bacon and garlic butter.

SCHNITTE: A slice or a piece, or a dish of, as well as meaning cold cuts.

SCHWARTENMAGEN: Parts of pig's head and stomach in aspic usually formed into a loaf with blood added to give it dark red color—a type of headcheese.

SCHWARZER und WEISSER PRESSACK: Bavarian pork headcheese of mixed dark and light meat in aspic.

SCHWARZGERÄUCHERTER: Dark-smoked.

SCHWARZGERÄUCHERTES: Pieces of dark-smoked ham or pork.

SCHWEDENBRÖTCHEN: Swedish plate of open-faced sandwiches.

SCHWEDENPLATTE: Swedish smorgasbord plate of mixed appetizers.

25

SCHWEDISCHE VORSPEISEN: Swedish smorgasbord plate with mixed appetizers, such as meat, fish, seafood, eggs with mayonnaise, marinated vegetables and cheese.

SCHWEIN(E)-: Pork.

    Braten: Cold roast pork.

    Kopfsülze: Pieces of cooked pig's head, feet and tail in aspic, a type of headcheese.

    Leberkäse: Meat loaf made of pig's liver, pork, bacon, seasoned with herbs.

    Pressack: A pork meat loaf, usually with some gelatin in it.

    Sülze: Pork head cheese.

SEMMELKNÖDEL mit EIER: Bread dumplings made with eggs.

SETZEI: Fried egg.

SHRIMPSALAT: Shrimp salad.

SOSSE: Sauce.

SPARGEL-: Asparagus (White).

    Spitzen: Tips.

SPECK: Bacon.

SPIEGELEI: Fried egg.

STADTWURST-SÜLZE: Any locally-made sausage in aspic.

STANGENSPARGEL: Asparagus spears.

STEINBUTTSALAT: Salad made of cold boiled turbot, similar to halibut.

STEINHUDER RÄUCHERAAL: Smoked eel from Steinhuder Lake region near Hanover.

STRAMMER MAX: "Strong Max"–a sandwich made of thick slice of cold ham on buttered dark bread, topped with fried egg.

STREICH: Soft, spreadable as butter.

STÜCK: Piece or portion.

SÜLZE: Aspic, small pieces of meat in aspic such as headcheese.

SÜLZKOTELETTE: Pork chop in aspic.

TARTAR (TATAR): Raw finely ground beef with garnish.

TARTARBEEFSTEAK mit EI: Raw finely ground beef with raw egg mixed in, garnished with chopped onions anchovies, capers and parsley.

TELLER: Plate.

TEUFELSSALAT: A salad with a spicy, vinegar dressing.

THUNFISCH: Tuna fish.

    "Aurora": With a tomato-flavored sauce.

TIEFSEEKREBSFLEISCH: Deep sea crayfish meat.

TOAST: Toasted bread.
TOMATEN: Tomatoes.
  mit **Feiner Fleischfüllung:** Stuffed with delicate meat filling.
  mit **Fleischsalat gefüllt:** Stuffed with cold meat salad.
  mit **Geflügelsalat gefüllt:** Stuffed with chicken salad.
TOMATENSAFT: Tomato juice.
TUNKE: Sauce.
ÜBERBACKEN: Put under the broiler.
ÜBERKRUSTEN: Cooked in very hot oven until browned on top.
ÜBERZOGEN: Covered with, coated or basted.
VERLORENE EIER BENEDIKT: Eggs Benedict—poached eggs put on toast on top of slice of ham, and covered with a cream sauce, usually Hollandaise.
WEINBERGSCHNECKEN: Burgundy snails.
  mit **Knoblauchbutter:** With garlic butter.
  mit **Kräuterbutter:** With herbal butter.
WEISSKOHL-EINTOPF mit SCHWEINSPFÖTCHEN: Cabbage casserole with pig's feet.
WESTFÄLISCHER SCHINKEN: The famous Westphalian raw-cured ham.
WIENER: From Vienna, or Vienna style.
WURST: Sausage.
WÜRSTCHEN: Meaning small sausages, such as hot dogs.
WURSTPLATTE: Plate of mixed sausages.
WURSTSALAT: Salad made with strips of sausage, vegetables, mayonnaise.
ZERLASSENE(R) BUTTER: Melted butter.
ZITRONE: Lemon.
ZWIEBEL(N)-: Onions.
    Ringe(n): Onion rings.
ZUNGE: Tongue.

WÜRSTE
(Sausages)

Are listed in a separate category which follows.

WÜRSTE
(Sausages)

The Germans are unequalled as producers and consumers of sausages. The famous frankfurter or hot dog, such a familiar part of the American diet, is only one of more than 300 varieties of sausages made in Germany.

Large-sized sausages (WÜRSTE) are eaten cold sliced as we do salami, and those which are small in diameter (WÜRSTCHEN), though they may be a foot long, are grilled, fried, boiled or braised, and are eaten with bread or rolls, or served with such accompaniments as sauerkraut or potato salad.

A delightful German institution is the streetside sausage stand where two or three different types of sausages crowd the grill from morning until late at night. They are served hot from the grill with mustard and a small white roll, the sausage often being three times the length of the roll. A glass of beer is the usual accompaniment.

The large railway stations will have several sausage stands where people in a hurry want something to eat and drink without taking the time to be seated at a table.

If you like hot dogs you cannot go wrong tasting almost any type of sausage, for while there are subtle taste differences in them, they are not highly spiced or strong-flavored. The following is a list of some of the most commonly offered sausages.

BIERWURST: A dried, medium-sized cooked salami stick, eaten cold.

BLUTWURST: Blood sausage, served hot.

BOCKWURST: A red skinned sausage—a hot dog, or can be a pigtail-size white sausage, both boiled.

BRATWURST: Means fry sausage. Can be from pigtail size to jumbos, and are usually of pork, whitish gray in color, and can be beautifully spiced. Different varieties carry the city or area name. Served grilled.

BRIESMILZWURST: Made of veal sweetbreads.

FLEISCHWURST: Same as Lyoner, but not in ring form.

FRANKFURTER: Hot dog, usually boiled. From Frankfort, this is the source of the name of the original American hot dog.

GRIEBENWURST: One in which large cubes of fat are used, as in blood sausage.

JAGDWURST: A smoked cooked sausage of pork, beef and bacon, served sliced.

KALBSBRATWURST: A white one of veal meat. Grilled.

KNACK(ER)WURST: A mildly spiced hot dog of pork and beef.

KNACKWURST: A very slightly garlic-flavored hot dog, usually boiled.

KNOCKWURST: A short, stubby fat hot dog, boiled or grilled.

LEBERWURST: Liverwurst.

LUFTTROCKENMETTWURST: Air-dried mettwurst.

LYONER: Similar to baloney. Comes ring-shaped. Served hot boiled, or grilled, or cold.

METTWURST: A cold cooked sausage that is soft and is spread on bread, but some varieties of mettwurst are harder and are sliced.

NÜRNBERGER: Small, pinkish colored, usually six to a serving. Grilled.

PFÄLZER: Hot dog type sausage from Pfalz.

PINKELWURST: Slender, bacon fat and oatmeal sausage, rather spicy, served boiled.

REGENSBURGER: A short, thick hot dog—a knockwurst which is boiled or grilled.

RIESENBOCKWURST: A very large hot dog.

RINDSWURST: Same as Kalbsbratwurst, but made of beef.

SAITENWURST: Hot dog type.

SCHINKENWURST: Pieces of ham in a pork baloney filling, eaten cold.

SCHWARTENMAGEN: Mildly spiced pork meat, fat, blood in gelatin—eaten cold.

SCHWEINSWÜRSTL: Small pork sausages, usually grilled.

STADTWURST: Means the sausage of a given city. Several types, but usually it is a long grey sausage, grilled.

STREICHWÜRSTE: Very soft, fine-grained sausage.

WIENER WÜRSTCHEN: Small Vienna style hot dogs, usually boiled.

WIENER WÜRSTL: Same as above.

WEISSWURST: Frequently Münchner—the Munich white sausage made of veal and flavored with parsley. Served boiled.

WOLLWURST: A mild white veal sausage without skin and in the form of a small meatloaf. Grilled.

WÜRSTCHEN: Hot dogs.

ZUNGENWURST: Made of pork blood with bits of tongue and diced fat. Eaten cold, sliced.

EIERSPEISEN und MEHLSPEISEN
(Egg and flour-made dishes)

Egg and flour-made dishes are often listed separately on German menus, as well as under the entrees, for they frequently constitute a complete light meal, being served often with potatoes, ham, vegetables and a small salad.

Breakfast eggs are usually soft-boiled, but all methods of preparing eggs are employed such as fried, poached, scrambled, hard-boiled. A variety of omelettes are offered, both sweet, with jam or stewed fruit, or with mushrooms, ham, bacon, cheese, herbs, chicken livers.

A counterpart to the omelette is the popular German Pfannkuchen, a large egg pancake served plain (NATUR) or with various fillings (GEFÜLLT) such as stewed fruit, bacon, cheese. Another version of the Pfannkuchen is the KAISERSCHMARRN, a type of flat pancake-omelette served with stewed fruit or applesauce, either as a light dish or a dessert.

The number of eggs served or used in the preparation of a given dish is indicated by "2-3 STÜCK"—two or three pieces (eggs).

APFEL-BEIGNETS: Apple fritters.

APFELSCHMARRN: Egg pancake with diced apples put into the dough.

EI(ER): Eggs.

> **Gebackene:** Fried in lots of butter or oil. Basted.
>
> **Geformte:** Put into a mold and poached in a tray of hot water.
>
> **Gefüllte:** Stuffed.
>
> **Hartgekochte:** Hard-boiled.
>
> in **Näpfen:** Shirred—put into individual containers and baked in the oven.
>
> **Pochierte:** Poached.
>
> **Rühreier:** Scrambled.
>
> mit **Aal:** With eel.
>
> mit **Champignons:** With mushrooms.
>
> mit **Edelpilzen:** With fine quality mushrooms.
>
> mit **Räucheraal:** With smoked eel.
>
> mit **Schinken:** With ham.
>
> **Setzei:** Fried egg.
>
> **Spiegelei:** Fried egg.
>
>> **"Bauern Art":** Peasant-style with bacon, potatoes and onions.

EI(ER):

    Spiegelei: (cont.)

  mit **Pfifferlingen:** With mushrooms.

  mit **Schinken:** With ham.

  mit **Spinat:** With spinach.

  Verlorene: Poached.

    of **Benedict mit Schinken au gratin:** Eggs Benedict
–poached eggs on toasted round of bread with slice of
ham on it, covered with Hollandaise sauce, put under
the broiler.

    Wachsweiche: Medium-boiled (5–6 min.). Favored
by most Germans for breakfast.

    Weichgekochte: Soft-boiled (3–4 min.).

EIERKUCHEN: Egg pancakes.

EIERPFANNKUCHEN: Egg pancakes.

  mit **Äpfeln:** With stewed apples, sprinkled with sugar
and cinnamon.

  mit **Kompott:** With stewed fruit.

  mit **Speck:** With bacon.

EIERTEIGWAREN: Egg noodles.

KAISERSCHMARRN: A type of flat pancake-omelette, made
of flour, milk, eggs, sprinkled with sugar and served
with stewed fruit. Sometimes a dessert, but usually a
light dish.

  mit **Apfelmus:** With applesauce.

KRÄUTEROMELETTE: Omelette with finely chopped green
herbs.

  mit **Champignons:** With mushrooms.

NUDELN: Noodles.

NUDELOMELETTE: An omelette filled with noodles mixed
with a sauce or butter and cheese, and/or ham—a
SCHINKENNUDELN-OMELETTE.

  mit **Tomatensauce:** With tomato sauce.

OMELETTE: Omelette.

    Bauernomelette: Peasant-style—with chopped bacon,
potatoes, onions.

  mit **Champignons:** With mushrooms.

  mit **Edelchampignons in Rahm:** With fine quality
mushrooms in a cream sauce.

  mit **Feinem Kalbfleischragout:** With diced veal parts in
a rich brown cream sauce.

  mit **Feinem Ragout:** Same as above.

  mit **"Fines Herbes":** With finely chopped parsley,
chervil, tarragon and chives.

  mit **Geflügelleber:** With sauteed chicken livers.

OMELETTE: (cont.)

    Gefüllt: A filled omelette.

    "Jäger Art": Hunter style filling of sauteed chicken livers and sliced mushrooms in a sauce.

mit **Konfitüre:** With jam.

    "Königin Art" mit Feinem Ragout: Queen-style–filled with diced chicken in a rich cream sauce.

mit **Leber:** With sauteed chopped liver.

    Natur: Plain.

    Nierchen Sauer: With finely chopped sauteed kidneys in a sour sauce.

    Nieren: With sauteed chopped kidneys.

mit **Parmesan:** With Parmesan cheese.

mit **Pilzen:** With mushrooms.

mit **Scallops:** With sauteed scallops.

mit **Schinken:** With ham.

    Souffle: Made with egg whites beaten separately and folded into yolks.

    Spanisches Omelette: Filling or sauce usually containing sauteed tomatoes and onions.

mit **Spargel:** With asparagus.

mit **Tomaten:** With stewed tomatoes.

PFANNKUCHEN: Egg pancake.

    Gefüllt: Filled.

mit **Käse:** With cheese.

    Natur: Plain.

mit **Speck:** With bacon.

SPECKPFANNKUCHEN: Egg pancake with bacon.

TEIGWAREN: Noodles.

TOAST (auf): Served on toast.

SUPPEN
(Soups)

Soups are a staple part of the German diet, served both hot and cold. The stocks from which most of them are made derive from either FLEISCHBRÜHE or BOUILLON (meat broth or bouillon), GEFLÜGELBRÜHE or HÜHNERBRÜHE (chicken broth) or HÜHNERBOUILLON (chicken bouillon), or FISCHBRÜHE (fish broth).

These basic stocks can be either KLARE (clear) or GEBUNDENE (thickened). The clear soup is a simple bouillon of any of the above, or it is a KRAFTBRÜHE (consomme) when the stock is made stronger by addition of lean meat and some vegetables, boiled down and strained. It is sometimes listed as DOPPELTE FLEISCH-BRÜHE (double bouillon).

A variety of additions to clear soups include noodles, rice, all types of dumplings, tiny ravioli, barley, bread, beaten eggs, pieces of seafood, fowl or meat, and various vegetables.

There are the traditional CREME or RAHM (cream) or PÜREE (pureed) soups such as cream of tomato, asparagus, mushroom, cauliflower, and lentil, split-pea and potato.

Also there are soups, served both hot and cold, such as WEINSUPPE (a liquid base of wine and water), or BIER-SUPPE (a liquid base of beer and water), made with many different ingredients, including fruit. The most common cold soup in this category is a summer specialty listed as KALTSCHALE or FRUCHTKALTSCHALE, which can be made of any fruit from apricots to strawberries in a white wine base.

A few well-known soups of foreign origin appear frequently on German menus such as ''Shark's Fin'', ''Kangerootail'', ''Bird's Nest'', ''Turtle''—all of which are canned or packaged.

Two hearty regional specialties that fall into the soup category, though often served as a main course, are AALSUPPE from Hamburg (an eel soup), and GAIS-BURGER MARSCH from Stuttgart (a beef and noodle soup).

Apart from soups of this type, any one of the above soups can appear on a menu as the TAGESSUPPE (soup of the day), and some restaurants with fixed price meals (GEDECK), offer a choice of soup under SUPPE NACH WAHL (soup of your choice).

The phrase MIT EINLAGE means that something is added to a clear soup. When preceded by another word such as MIT FLEISCHEINLAGE, it tells you specifically what has been added, in this case meat.

Soups which are a specialty of certain regions will be preceded by the regional name such as HAMBURGER HUMMERSUPPE (a lobster soup from Hamburg), SCHWÄBISCHE KARTOFFELSUPPE (a potato soup from Swabia), or MÜNCHENER LEBERKNÖDELSUPPE (a liver dumpling soup from Munich).

A frequent accompaniment to soups are KÄSESTANGEN (cheese straws made of pastry dough), or CHESTERSTANGEN (Cheddar-cheese straws).

AALSUPPE: A Hamburg specialty. It is a sweet-sour soup containing pieces of boiled fresh eel, whole prunes and other dried fruits in a broth flavored with white wine, ham or bacon, vegetables and spices.

BACKERBSENSUPPE: Pea-sized balls of pancake dough which are deep-fried and added to bouillon.

BAUERNSUPPE: Peasant style—a vegetable-based soup.

BAYRISCHE LEBERKNÖDELSUPPE: Bavarian liver dumpling soup.

BIERSUPPE: Soup made with liquid base of beer with spices added.

BLUMENKOHLKREMSUPPE: Cream of cauliflower soup.

BOHNENSUPPE: Bean soup.

BOUILLABAISSE "MARSEILLER ART": The famous Marseilles fish soup-stew.

BOUILLON: Bouillon or broth.

mit **Ei:** With beaten egg added.

mit **Mark:** With marrow added.

mit **Markklösschen:** With marrow dumplings added.

BROTSUPPE: A soup which includes pieces of bread, usually rye, cooked together with various vegetables and flavorings.

mit **Röstzwiebel:** With sauteed or fried onions added.

BRÜHE: Bouillon or broth.

CHAMPIGNONCREMESUPPE: Cream of mushroom soup.

CHAMPIGNONRAHMSUPPE: Same as above.

CHESTERSTANGEN: Cheddar-cheese straws served with soup.

CONSOMME: Strengthened bouillon.

CREME: Creamed.

DOPPELTE KRAFTBRÜHE: Double bouillon or consomme.

ECHTE SCHILDKRÖTENSUPPE: Genuine turtle soup.

EIEREINLAUF: Beaten egg added to bouillon.

EIERFLOCKENSUPPE: Like Chinese egg-drop soup, beaten eggs and flour poured into boiling bouillon and stirred to form little flakes.

EINLAGE(N): Something added to a clear soup.
    Feine: Fine, delicate addition.

EINLAUFSUPPE: Like Chinese egg-drop soup, beaten eggs and flour poured into boiling bouillon and stirred to form long threads.

ERBSENSUPPE: Pea soup.

FISCHSUPPE: Fish soup.

FISCHRAHMSUPPE: A creamed fish soup.

FLÄDLESUPPE: A hot bouillon to which thin strips of pancake are added.

FLEISCH: Meat.

FLEISCHBRÜHE: Meat broth or bouillon.
    mit **Ei:** With beaten egg added.
    mit **Leberknödel:** With liver dumplings.
    mit **Mark:** With marrow.
    mit **Markklösschen:** With marrow dumplings.
    mit **Maultaschen:** Small raviolis filled with chopped meat, spinach, egg, bread.
        Natur: Plain.
    mit **Rindermark:** With beef marrow.

FRÄNKISCHE BROTSUPPE: Upper Bavarian bread soup.

FRANZÖSISCHE FISCHSUPPE: French fish soup, probably "Bouillabaisse".
    Hummersuppe: French lobster soup.
    Zwiebelsuppe: French onion soup.

FRUCHTKALTSCHALE: Sugared and pureed fruits and flavorings added to a soup with a white wine base. Normally served chilled.

FRÜHLINGSSUPPE: Spring vegetable soup.

GAISBURGER MARSCH: A Stuttgart specialty. It is a beef and noodle soup, heavily laden with cubed boiling beef, potatoes, sliced onions and homemade noodles.

GAZPACHO: A spanish vegetable soup served cold.

GEBUNDEN(E): Thickened.

GEFLÜGEL: Chicken.

GEFLÜGELCREMESUPPE: Cream of chicken soup.

GELBE ERBSENSUPPE: Dried yellow pea soup.

GEMÜSESUPPE: Vegetable soup.

GERSTENSUPPE: Barley soup.

GOULASCHSUPPE (GULASCHSUPPE): Goulash soup.

GRIESSKLOSSUPPE: A bouillon with small dumplings made of semolina (inner kernel of hard durum wheat ground into a semi-fine flour).

GRIESSNOCKERLSUPPE: Same as above.

GRIESSUPPE: Soup containing semolina.

GRÜNKERNSUPPE: German wheat picked before it is ripe, peeled, then put into soup–similar to barley.

GURKENSUPPE: Cucumber soup.

HAFERSCHLEIMSUPPE: Oats boiled in salted water, similar to Scotch porridge.

HAIFISCHFLOSSENSUPPE: Shark's fin soup (canned).

HAMBURGER AALSUPPE: Famous specialty of Hamburg, an eel soup (see AALSUPPE).

    Hummersuppe: Hamburg lobster soup.

    Krebssuppe: Hamburg crayfish soup.

HAMMELBOUILLON: Mutton broth.

HOCHZEITSUPPE: A wedding soup, an elaborate, rich soup with many combinations of ingredients, including meats and vegetables.

HÜHN(ER): Chicken.

    Bouillon: Chicken broth.

    Brühe: Chicken bouillon.

    Cremesuppe: Cream of chicken soup.

    Kraftbrühe: Chicken consomme.

    Suppe: Chicken soup.

HUMMER-: Lobster.

    Cremesuppe: Cream of lobster soup.

    Rahmsuppe: Same as above.

    Suppe: Lobster soup.

INDISCHE REISCREMESUPPE: Indian rice cream soup.

    Trapangsuppe: Made from smoked sea cucumber (see TRAPANGSUPPE).

JULIENNESUPPE mit SAGO: Vegetable soup with tapioca added.

KALBFLEISCHRAHMSUPPE: A cream soup which includes cooked veal.

KALBFLEISCHSUPPE: A clear soup which includes cooked veal.

KALTSCHALE or FRUCHTKALTSCHALE: Sugared, pureed fruits added to a soup with a white wine base. Normally served chilled.

    Aprikosen: With apricots.

    Erdbeeren: With strawberries.

    Kirschen: With cherries.

KÄNGURUHSCHWANZSUPPE: Kangaroo-tail soup (canned).

KÄNGURUHSUPPE: Same as above.

KAROTTENSUPPE: Carrot soup.

KARTOFFELSUPPE: Potato soup.

KÄSESTANGEN: Cheese straws made of pastry dough, served with soup.

KERBELSUPPE: Medium thick potato soup with small pieces of meat and chopped chervil.

KLARE: Clear soup–a broth.

KOHLSUPPE: Cabbage soup.

KÖNIGINSUPPE: Cream of chicken soup with rice.

KRAFTBRÜHE: Consomme.

  mit **Ei:** With beaten egg added.

  mit **Fadennudeln:** With string noodles.

  mit **Flädle:** With thin strips of pancake added.

  mit **Leberknödel:** With liver dumplings.

  mit **Leberspätzle:** Same as above.

  mit **Mark:** With marrow.

  mit **Nudeln:** With noodles.

  mit **Omeletten:** With beaten eggs cooked as an omelette, then cut into very thin strips and added to the soup.

KRÄUTERSUPPE: Soup flavored with chopped herbs.

KRAUTSUPPE: Cabbage soup.

KREBSSUPPE: Crayfish soup.

KREM: Creamed.

LAUCHCREMESUPPE: Leek soup.

LEBERKLOSSUPPE: Liver dumpling soup.

LEBERKNOCKERLSUPPE: With flour dumplings which include scraped chicken or calf liver mixed with chopped onions and parsley. These dumplings can also be a main dish when served with a sauce.

LEBERKNÖDELSUPPE: Munich or Bavarian specialty– dumplings of minced liver, bread, onions and spices served in bouillon.

LEGIERTE: Thickened.

LINSENSUPPE: Lentil soup.

MARKKLOSSUPPE: Marrow dumpling soup.

MARK: Marrow.

MÜNCHNER LEBERKNÖDELSUPPE: Famous Munich liver dumpling soup.

MUSCHELSUPPE: Mussel soup.

NUDELSUPPE: Consomme with noodles.

  mit **Huhn:** Chicken and noodle soup.

NUDELSUPPE: (cont.)

mit **Hühnermagen:** Chicken giblets and noodle soup.

OCHSENSCHWANZSUPPE: Oxtail soup.

Gebundene mit Madeira: Thickened and flavored with Madeira wine.

mit **Klößchen:** With dumplings.

mit **Pilzen:** With mushrooms.

mit **Sherry:** With sherry wine added.

PFANNKUCHENSUPPE: A hot bouillon to which thin strips of pancake are added.

REISSUPPE: Broth with rice cooked in it.

RAHM: Creamed.

RIND(ER): Beef.

RINDFLEISCHSUPPE: Soup made with boiled beef.

RUMFORDSUPPE: Dried yellow pea soup with pearl barley, diced potatoes and fried bacon diced.

SAHNE: Creamed.

SCHILDKRÖTENSUPPE: Turtle soup (canned).

"Lady Curzon": Turtle soup flavored with curry powder and topped with a whipped cream garnish.

SCHNECKENSUPPE in CURRYRAHM: A cream soup flavored with curry powder with snails added.

SCHOTTISCHE KRAFTBRÜHE: Scotch broth made with diced mutton.

SCHWALBENNESTERSUPPE: Bird's nest soup (canned).

SELLERIECREMESUPPE: Cream of celery soup.

SPARGELCREMESUPPE: Cream of asparagus soup.

SPINATCREMESUPPE: Cream of spinach soup.

SUPPE HAUSGEMACHT: Homemade soup.

SUPPE NACH WAHL: Soup of your choice.

SUPPENHUHNTOPF: Chicken soup casserole dish.

SUPPENMAKRONEN: Macaroons made of beaten egg white, sugar, finely ground almonds, baked and added to soups.

TAGESSUPPE: Soup of the day.

TASSE: Cup.

TELLER: Dish or soup dish.

TERRINE: Terrine or large bowl.

TOMATENCREMESUPPE: Cream of tomato soup.

TOMATENKRAFTBRÜHE: Consomme flavored with tomatoes.

TOMATENSUPPE: Tomato soup.

TRAPANGSUPPE: A Malay dish made from a smoked fried sea cucumber which is boiled and served in broth.

TRÜFFELKRAFTBRÜHE: Consomme garnished with truffles.

WALSUPPE: Whale soup.

WEINSUPPE: Soup made of a liquid base of wine.

WEISSE WINDSORSUPPE: A cream soup with rice, veal, seasonings.

ZWIEBELSUPPE: Onion soup.

　　Französisch: Parisian or French onion soup.

FISCHGERICHTE
(Fish Dishes)

The German menu will normally include several types of fish well-known to us such as FORELLE (trout), SEE-ZUNGE (sole), HEILBUTT (halibut), SALM or LACHS (salmon), SCHELLFISCH (haddock), STEINBUTT (turbot), BARSCH (perch).

It will also include others not normally served in our restaurants such as HECHT (pike), KARPFEN (carp), SCHLEIE (tench), SCHOLLEN (plaice), and of course, AAL (eel), a great German favorite.

The two most popular methods of preparing fish are BLAU (boiled), especially trout taken live (LEBENDER) from a fish tank (BASSIN) in the restaurant, or "MÜLLERIN ART"—Miller's wife's style, which is dredged in flour, and fried in butter and oil.

HERING (herring) you will find everywhere in Germany. It is used for sandwiches and salads and is prepared in many different ways, but an especially well-known herring dish served as a first course is "MATJESHERINGSFILET" "HAUSFRAUEN ART" or Housewife's style. These are filets of salt-cured young herring served with slices of onion, apple, cucumber, pickle, tomato, usually in, or with a rich sour cream sauce.

MEERESFRÜCHTE (seafood) will include AUSTERN (oysters), KREBS or KRABBEN (crayfish or prawns), LANGUSTEN (California lobster), HUMMER (lobster), MUSCHELN (mussels) and JAKOBSMUSCHELN (scallops), all served much the same way we do.

AAL: Eel.

    Blau: Blue, meaning boiled, with a little salt and vinegar.

    Grün: Served cold after being poached in white wine or vinegar, then covered with a sauce made from poaching liquid thickened with egg yolk, or served with a green-colored herbal butter or a dill sauce.

    Steinhuder: Eel from Steinhuder Lake area.

ALSE: Shad.

ANGELSCHELLFISCH: Individually line and hook caught haddock, as opposed to net-caught.

AUSTERN: Oysters.

    Holländische: From Holland.

BACHFORELLE: Stream-raised trout.

41

BARSCH: Perch, either fresh water or sea.

BASSIN: Live fish tank.

BLAU: Blue, meaning boiled.

BLAUFELCHEN: Blue whitefish, a variety of fresh water whitefish.

BRATHERING: Floured herring, fried, then marinated in a sauce of onions, vinegar and sour cream; served cold.

DILLSAUCE: A white sauce with chopped dill weed and other herbs.

DONAUWALLER: Catfish from Danube River.

DORSCH: Codfish.

    Hiesiger: Local or native cod.

    Rogen: Codfish roe.

ECHTE(R): Genuine.

FELCHEN: A fresh water whitefish, as Lake Michigan whitefish.

FISCHRAGOUT: A fish stew.

FISCHLI: Meaning little fish. Could be any little whitebait sort of fish.

FLUSSKARPFEN: River carp.

FORELLE(N): Trout.

    Frankenweinsud: Served in a creamed white wine sauce.

    Lebensfrische: Living fresh, meaning taken fresh and alive from the restaurant's live fish tank.

    "Müllerin Art": A renowned method of cooking trout and sole (see "Müllerin Art").

    Regenbogen: Rainbow trout.

FRISCHE(R): Fresh.

FROSCHSCHENKEL: Frog legs.

GANZ(E): Whole, entire, as a whole fish.

GEBACKEN: Usually means fried or deep-fried for fish, but can mean baked.

GEBRATEN: Usually means fried for fish, but has a general sense of meaning cooked.

GEKOCHT(ER)(ES): Boiled.

GERÄUCHERTE(S)(R): Smoked.

GESOTTEN: Simmered, or boiled.

GOLDBARSCH: Red seabass, an Atlantic fish of perch-like appearance. Resembles a red snapper.

GOLDBUTT: The Brill, a flat sole-like fish, similar to the turbot.

GRANAT: Shrimp.

GRILL (vom): Grilled.

GRÜN: A sauce made from liquid in which fish is poached,

42

GRÜN: (cont.)
then thickened with egg yolk and flavored with lemon juice and chopped green herbs.

HAIFISCH: Shark steak.

HECHT: Pike, a fresh water fish.

HEILBUTT: Halibut.

HERING: Herring.

HIESIGER: Local or native.

HOLLANDAISE SAUCE: The French sauce made with butter, egg yolks and lemon juice.

HUMMER: Lobster, true lobster with claws.

HUMMERKRABBEN: Large prawns.

JAKOBSMUSCHELN: Scallops.

KABELJAU: Cod, codfish.

    Kutterkabeljau: Cutter-caught (a small boat) codfish.

KAISERKRABBEN: Special, high quality shrimps.

KARPFEN: Carp.

    Spiegelkarpfen: A variety of carp.

KRABBEN: Shrimps.

    Büsumer: From Busum on the North Sea coast.

KRÄUTERBUTTER: Herbal butter.

KREBS(E)-: Freshwater crayfish or crawdads.

    Fleisch: Crayfish meat.

    Schwänze: Crayfish tails.

KUMMELSUD: Poaching liquid flavored with caraway seeds.

LACHS: Salmon.

LACHS-SALM: Salmon.

LANGUSTEN-: Spiny lobster, no claws. The California, or South African type.

    Schwänze: Lobster tails.

-EBENSFRISCHE: Living fresh, meaning taken fresh and alive from the restaurant's live fish tank.

-ENGFISCHFILET: Filet of ling cod.

-AINFISCHLI: Little fish from the Main River.

-AKRELE: Mackerel.

-ATJESHERINGSFILET: Filets of young female herring which has not yet spawned.

    "Hausfrauenart": Housewife's style—filets of salt-cured young herring, served cold with sliced onions, apples, pickles, tomatoes; in, or with a sour cream sauce.

-EER: Sea.

-EERESFRÜCHTE: Seafood.

MÜLLERIN ART": Miller's wife's style—about the most frequently encountered preparation for various fish in

"MÜLLERIN ART": (cont.)

Germany; dredged in flour, and fried in butter and oil.

MUSCHELN: Mussels, the dark-bluish shelled, clam-like mollusc with orange meat.

> **Spanische in Sherryweinsoße:** Spanish mussels in Sherry wine sauce.

PANIERT(E): Breaded.

POCHIERT(E): Poached.

RÄUCHERAAL: Smoked eel.

RAUCHSALM: Smoked salmon.

REGENBOGENFORELLE(N): Rainbow trout.

RENKE: Whitefish, fresh water, as a Lake Michigan whitefish.

REMOULADENSAUCE: Mayonnaise sauce with mustard, anchovies, capers, gherkins, tarragon, chervil.

ROGEN: Roe.

ROST (vom): Grilled.

ROTBARSCHFILET: Filets of red seabass.

ROTZUNGE: Lemon sole, similar to a sanddab.

SAHNEMEERRETTICH: Horseradish cream sauce.

SALBEI: Sage.

SALM: Another name for salmon.

> **Nordischer Rauchsalm:** Northern smoked salmon.

SAUCE: Sauce.

SCAMPI: Prawns.

> **Königscampi:** Scampi or medium-sized prawns.
>
> **Riesenscampi:** Large prawns.

SCHELLFISCH: Haddock.

SCHLEIE: Tench, a small fresh water member of the carp family—like a goldfish.

SCHNITTE: A slice of.

SCHOLLEN: Plaice, a horizontally flat fish of the flounder family.

SCHWÄNZE: Tails.

SEELACHS: Called a sea salmon, but it is a coalfish or rock salmon with an olive green skin and is similar to the codfish.

SEEZUNGE: Sole. The Germans recognize nearly 400 different, named methods of preparing sole. The fancier and more elegant the restaurant the more varied names of preparations you are likely to encounter. We list only a few.

> **"Colbert":** A rather frequently encountered preparation. Semi-fileted, floured, egg-dipped, breaded, fried

SEEZUNGE:

    "Colbert": (cont.)

in butter; bone removed and fish served with a pocket filled with herbal butter wine sauce– the Colbert sauce.

    Gebacken: Fried. Usually filets, and may be breaded and deep-fried as well.

    "Müllerin Art": Miller's wife's style–dredged in flour and fried in butter and oil.

    Röllchen: Rolled filets stuffed or not; usually poached in white wine or fish stock; served in a myriad of different sauces.

SENFTUNKE: Mustard sauce.

SOLOKREBS: Individual large prawns.

SOSSE: Sauce.

SPIESS (am): On a skewer.

SPROTTEN: Sprats, a small herring-like seafish.

    Kieler: Sprats from Kiel.

STEINBEISSER: Seawolf, frequently smoked. It is also called a sea catfish.

STEINBUTT: Turbot, a medium large flat seafish. Closest U.S. fish is halibut.

STÖR: Sturgeon, the fish from which caviar comes.

    Geräuchert: Smoked.

    Seestörsteak: Sturgeon steak.

SUD (im): Poached in broth or other liquid.

TAFEL: Suitable for the table or choice.

TARTAR-SAUCE: Mayonnaise with chopped onion, capers, herbs.

TINTENFISCH: Cuttlefish, similar to squid.

THUNFISCH: Tuna fish.

    "Griechische Art": Greek style-slices poached in and served cold in herbal brew with lemon juice, oil.

TOMATEN-SAUCE: Tomato sauce.

TUNKE: Sauce.

WALLER: Catfish, can be up to 400 lbs.

WEINSUD: Sauce made from wine fish stock.

WEISSWEIN: White wine.

WÜRZELSUD: Pickling brew.

ZANDER: Pike-perch, a fresh water river fish.

ZERLASSENER BUTTER: Melted butter.

ZITRONE: Lemon.

HAUPTGERICHTE
(Main Courses)

These are the main courses, or meat courses or dishes. They will be found listed under any of the following names and are translated in this section:

FERTIGE SPEISEN: Ready-cooked, or ready to serve dishes.

FLEISCHGERICHTE: Meat dishes.

GRILLGERICHTE: Grilled meat dishes.

KALTE SPEISEN: Cold main dishes.

SPEZIALITÄTEN: Specialties of the house.

VOM GRILL: Dishes from the grill.

VOM HAMMEL: Mutton dishes.

VOM LAMM: Lamb dishes.

VOM RIND: Beef main dishes.

VOM ROST: Main dishes grilled or roasted.

VOM SCHWEIN: Pork main dishes.

VOM SPIESS: Skewered dishes; can be from a spit.

WARME SPEISEN: Hot main dishes.

GEFLÜGEL und WILD
(Fowl and Wild Game)

These will be found listed immediately following the FLEISCHGERICHTE (meat dishes).

GEFLÜGEL: Fowl, both domestic and wild.

WILD: Wild game dishes, such as venison.

HAUPTGERICHTE
(Main Courses)

AUBERGINE, GEFÜLLTE mit Schinkenfarce überbacken: Eggplant with chopped ham stuffing, put under the broiler to brown.

BADISCHE KRAUTWICKEL: Cabbage roll stuffed with various meat and spice combinations, with or without rice.

BAUCHFLEISCH: Belly meat (pork), the part from which bacon is made, either pickled or fresh. Served in thick slices, boiled.

BAUERNSCHMAUS: Farmer's Feast—a copious plate of cooked pork, sausage, bacon, sauerkraut, mashed potatoes and dumplings.

BAYERISCHER LINSENTOPF mit Geräuchertem: Bavarian lentil casserole with smoked pork and spices.

BAYERISCH LEBERKNÖDEL: Bavarian dumpling, tennis ball size, containing chopped liver, bacon, onion.

BEEFSTEAK, DEUTSCHES (a la Meyer or Maier): This is the hamburger of Germany—a large, finely ground patty, fried, served with French fried onion rings, and pan-fried boiled potatoes.

BOCKWURST: A red-skinned sausage, a hot dog, or can be a pigtail-size white sausage, both boiled.

BRATEN: Roast.

BRATWURST: A whiteish to pinkish sausage of pork, mildly spiced, usually grilled. Popular everywhere, a number of varieties, as Nürnberger, Fränkisch, Bauern, but all are roughly of the same ingredients.

    Sülze Pikant: Pieces of boiled bratwurst in aspic with spices.

BREMER KÜCHENRAGOUT: A stew of young chicken, sweetbreads, calf meat balls, mussels, and asparagus, with thick sauce of cream, butter and egg.

BRÖSCHEN: Sweetbreads.

BURGUNDERSCHINKEN: Ham cooked in a white Burgundy wine, and served with mushrooms in Madeira wine sauce, or can be in red wine sauce with vegetables.

CHAMPIGNONS, SCHMORBRATEN: Pot roast braised with mushrooms.

CHEN: Diminutive suffix, meaning little or small.

CORDON BLEU: Two very thin veal cutlets with a slice of cooked ham and Swiss cheese between them; dipped in egg batter, breadcrumbs, and fried in butter.

CORDON ROUGE: Veal or beef filet with mushrooms, chicken livers and tarragon.

DEUTSCHES BEEFSTEAK: This is the hamburger of Germany—a large, finely ground patty, fried, served with French-fried onion rings, and pan-fried boiled potatoes.

EISBEIN: An ubiquitous cut, pork shanks (lower thigh above the knee) usually pickled, and served boiled with sauerkraut, and mashed potatoes. Can also be roasted fresh. We would call them pork hocks.

    in **Aspic:** Pickled, boiled, and served decorated cold in aspic (gelatin).

    Hausgepökeltes: Home, or house-pickled.

ENTRECOTE: Beef loin steak (as boneless T-bone).

FALSCHER HASE: False Hare—a meat loaf of seasoned

FALSCHER HASE: (cont.)

chopped beef, veal and pork, covered with a sauce of creamed pan juices.

FEIN(ER)(ES): Fine or delicate.

FILET GOULASCH "Stroganoff": Beef Stroganoff—tenderloin beef strips, cooked in a creamy gravy of onions, mushrooms, seasonings.

FILETSCHEIBEN "Art des Hauses": Style of the house—lean bacon, pineapple, curry powder and truffle sauce served on slices of beef filet.

FILETSTEAK: Beef tenderloin steak.

mit **Kräuterbutter:** Grilled and served topped with butter creamed with chopped herbs and lemon juice.

à la **Meyer:** Beef tenderloin fried in butter, and topped with fried onion rings.

FLEISCHKÄSE: A meat loaf. If BAYERISCHER (Bavarian), will be LEBERKÄSE.

FRANKFURTER: From Frankfort, or Frankfort style.

FRÄNKISCHE LEBERKLÖSSE in Specksauce: Franken liver dumplings in bacon sauce or gravy.

FRISCHE: Fresh.

FRIKADELLEN: Sort of croquettes; meat balls or reformed cutlets made of half beef, half pork, breaded, and then pan, or deep-fried.

GAISBURGER MARSCH: A Stuttgart specialty. A beef and noodle soup heavily laden with cubed boiling beef, potatoes, sliced onions and homemade noodles (Spätzle).

GEBACKEN or GEB.: Roasted, but usually means deep-fried or fried for meats, and baked for bread.

GEBRATEN or GEB.: Means fried, principally, but can also mean roasted or even braised. Has a general sense of meaning cooked.

GEFLÜGEL: Chicken. (See under GEFLÜGEL und WILD following).

GEFÜLLTE or GEF.: Means stuffed, as bell peppers cabbage leaves.

GERÖSTET: Roasted.

GESCHNETZELTES: Small cut tid-bits of veal.

in **Rahm:** In a cream sauce.

"**Schweizer Art":** Swiss style—fried, then served in a brown sauce of butter, flour-thickened, with white wine and sweet or sour cream added.

"**Zigeuner Art":** Gypsy style—same as above but with bell peppers, paprika, and mushrooms.

GESPICKTES: Larded; holes made in meat, and filled with strips of pork fat.

GOULASCH or GULASCH: Basically pieces of meat braised in a sauce or gravy. The Hungarian one being the one we know best, paprika being the identifying ingredient.

    "Szegediner": One variety of the Hungarian goulash, named after this city. Pork cubes browned in hot lard, braised in onions and paprika, and stewed with sauerkraut, sauce thickened with flour and cream.

    "Ungarischer" or Ung.: Basic Hungarian goulash. Fat-fried onions, paprika added, then cubed meat; then braised with water, vegetables added at the end. Germans include marjoram and carroway seed.

    "Zigeuner": Gypsy style—same as Hungarian with or without bell peppers.

GRILL (vom): Grilled.

GRILLTELLER: Plate of various cuts of grilled meats.

HACKBRATEN nach "Art des Hauses": House style—large size hamburger patty or meat loaf slices.

HACKRAHMSTEAK: Hamburger patty served topped with cream thickened brown gravy.

HACKSPIESSCHEN "Zigeuner Art": Gypsy style—small meat balls on skewer with bell peppers, tomatoes, onion.

HÄMCHEN: Pork hock or shank, usually corned, served with sauerkraut and potatoes.

HAMMEL-: Mutton (mature sheep).

    Keule: Leg of mutton.

    Kotelette: Mutton chop.

    Reisfleisch mit Paprikaschoten: Braised mutton with bell peppers, served in a rice ring.

    Schlegel: Leg or thigh of mutton.

HASE: Hare, a large-sized variety of rabbit.

HASENLÄUFE in Jägerrahmsauce: Hare thigh in Hunter's style dark cream sauce of mushrooms, shallots, white wine and chopped parsley.

HASENPFEFFER: The famous hare stew. Pieces of marinated hare braised in red wine, blood from the hare, and served in this sauce with mushrooms and onions.

HAXE: The hock or shank above or just below the knee. On veal it is the haxe; on pork, either Haxe or Eisbein.

    Grillhaxe: Fresh, grilled hock or shank.

HEIDSCHNUCKENKEULE: Leg of lamb from area S.E. of Hamburg (Luneburg Heath).

    in **Wacholderrahm:** In a juniper berry cream sauce.

HERZ-LEBER-NIERENSPIESSCHEN: Heart, liver and kidney grilled on skewer.

HERZLES PIKANTES TÖPFLE: A Swiss casserole dish of small pieces of veal heart in a seasoned brown gravy.

HIMMEL und ERDE: Heaven and Earth–combination of potatoes and apples or applesauce served with blood sausage.

HIRN mit RÜHREI "Wiener Art": Calves' brains with scrambled eggs, Vienna style.

HIRTENSTEAK: Shepherd's Steak–a veal steak with optional garnish.

HOLSTEIN-SCHNITZEL: Pan-fried veal cutlet topped with fried egg, and served, if classical, with garnish of pieces of toast covered with anchovies, mussels, smoked salmon, and vegetables. A widely offered dish.

HOLSTEINER mit Setzei: Same as above.

HÜFT(E): Top sirloin steak, beef or veal.

JÄGER-: A hunter, and JÄGER ART means Hunter's style.

> **Braten, "Schwäbischer":** Slices of roast pork in a velvety brown sauce with sliced mushrooms.

> **Schnitzel mit Pfifferlingen:** Hunter style veal cutlet fried, and served with a dark sauce of sliced mushrooms, chopped shallots, white wine, tomato sauce, tarragon and chervil.

> **Topf:** Hunter style casserole dish, or stew, of meat chunks, tomato sauce, shallots, tarragon.

JUNGE: Young.

JUNGE SCHWEINERÜCKEN: Roasted young pig's back loin, or saddle.

KALB(S)-: Calf, i. e., veal; after pork, the most offered meat in Germany.

> **Blatt:** Shoulder of veal.

> **Braten:** Roast leg or loin of veal.

> **Bratwürstchen, abgebräunt:** Grilled or pan-fried small whitish sausages of veal meat.

> **Bries, in Weißwein:** Calf sweetbreads poached in white wine sauce. There are many different preparations with their sauces (more than 117).

> **Bröschen:** Sweetbreads.

> **Brust Gefüllte or Gef.:** Boneless breast of veal, stuffed either with plain bread, or with added meats, as chicken livers, ham.

> **Filet:** Veal tenderloin, or filet steak.

> **Fleisch:** The word for flesh, or meat.

> **Fleischbällchen:** Small, round veal meatballs.

KALB(S): (cont.)

Fleischklößchen: Veal meatballs with suet, eggs, onions, spices; poached in water or stock.

Fleischragout (Feinem): Finely cut pieces of veal in a rich thickened brown sauce.

Fleischschnitte in Rahmsauce: Slice of veal in brown gravy enriched with cream.

Frikassee: Veal fricassee; cubed, floured, seared; then simmered in a brew with onions, herbs; final sauce thickened with egg yolk and cream.

Geschabtes: Scraped, minced, or finely ground veal made back into patties.

Geschnetzeltes: Small sliced morsels cooked in a thickened brown herbal sauce.

Goulasch: Braised pieces of veal with seasonings.

Haxe: The very popular veal hocks or shanks.

    Gebraten or Geb.: Baked or roasted.

    Knusprig Geb.: Crispy roasted veal shank.

Herz (vom Rost): Veal heart, cooked on mesh grill or gridiron; either broiled or baked.

Hirn mit Rührei: Calves' brains with scrambled eggs.

Kopf (Gebraten): Calf's head, boiled and boned, cut into squares, marinated in oil and lemon juice, dipped in batter and deep-fried.

    Kotelette: This is a veal chop.

    vom **Grill:** Grilled.

    "Jäger Art": Hunter style—fried in butter, served in a brown gravy of sliced mushrooms, shallots, white wine, tomato paste, chopped tarragon and chervil.

    vom **Rost:** Grilled or broiled.

Leber: Calf's liver.

    nach **"Berliner Art":** Berlin style—floured, fried in butter, and served topped with fat-fried onion rings and apple slices.

    Gebraten: Breaded and fried in butter.

Lendchen: Veal tenderloin, or filet.

    vom **Rost:** Grilled.

Lunge: Calf's lungs. Normally blanched and served in white cream sauce seasoned with lemon juice, bay leaf, sugar, peppercorns, and herbs.

Mast: Grain-fed.

Medaillons: Small diameter slices from upper leg (stripped-out tenderest ligaments of sirloin).

Milch: Sweetbreads.

KALB(S): (cont.)

Nierenbraten: Saddle of veal with kidney attached; can be boned and rolled.

Nüßchen: Sirloin tip of veal, usually internally larded and roasted.

Rahm: Meaning served with a rich, sweet, or sour cream enriched brown sauce or gravy.

Rollbraten: Rolled veal; large, flat piece rolled, tied, roasted. May be stuffed.

Rücken: Back, or loin of veal.

Saftgoulasch: Meaning juicy goulash. Veal stew with paprika, onions, tomato puree, meat stock; served with large amount of gravy.

Schlegel: Leg of veal.

Schnitzel: A veal cutlet, famous in Germany. There are many, many preparations. It is frequently listed merely as schnitzel.

Grilliert: Grilled.

"Jäger": (See under Jäger).

"Prinzess": Fried, served in mushroom sauce with garnish of potato croquettes, and patty shell filled with creamed asparagus tips.

"Russisch": Butter-fried with cream sauce, tomatoes, mushrooms, pickles, lemon juice, and topped with caviar.

"Sardellen": Served with anchovies in the sauce.

Wiener: The famous Vienna style cutlet—floured, egg-dipped, breaded, fried in lard, served with chopped parsley and lemon wedges (Austrian).

(For more preparations see under Schnitzel.)

Schulter: Veal shoulder.

Steak: Veal steak; from loin, rib, or leg. Many preparations; names for which involve the sauce or garnish served with it.

Vogerl: Veal cutlets stuffed and rolled; then pot-roasted with vegetables, white wine; gravy made of strained cooking liquid, with capers and anchovies added.

KASSELER: From Kassel in Hesse comes this renown treatment of whole, bone-in pork loins, first pickled, then smoked. It is eaten cold or hot, roasted or boiled, usually served with sauerkraut and potatoes.

Rippchen, Rippe, Ripperl, Rippenspeer, Rauchrücken: All are different names for the smoked pork rib loin chop.

KATENRAUCHSCHINKEN: Peasant-cottage style smoked ham.

KESSELFLEISCH: Freshly-killed pork meat originally cooked in large cauldron; now boiled and served with vegetable garnish.

KESSELGOULASCH: A goulash of pork meat freshly-killed.

KIMBURGER KOTELETTE: Cutlet formed of ground pork and veal, breaded and fried.

KOHLROULADE in RAHM: Cabbage roll in cream sauce. Stuffed rolled leaves simmered in broth.

KÖNIGSBERGER KLOPS: Large meat balls of pork, beef, veal, bread, onions, anchovies, lemon peel, parsley, cooked in seasoned water, and served with rich thick white sauce of sour cream, capers, butter, egg, lemon juice.

KOPFSÜLZE: Seasoned pork head-cheese loaf held together with gelatin (in aspic).

KOTELETTE: A chop, usually from rib in veal; from loin in pork.

KRÄUTERBUTTER: A lump of butter creamed with chopped herbs and lemon juice.

KRÄUTERSTEAK: Fried steak served with Kräuterbutter on top.

KRAUTWICKEL: Meat-mixture stuffed cabbage leaf rolls.

LABSKAUS: A fine grained hash of boiled potatoes, salt pork, herring; with beets, fried onions. A Hamburg specialty.

LAMM-: Lamb.
>   **Braten:** Roast leg of lamb.
>   **Irisches Lammgericht:** Irish stew of lamb.
>   **Kotelette vom Rost:** Broiled lamb chop.
>   **Schlegel:** Leg of lamb.

LEBER-: Liver.
>   **"Berliner Art":** Berlin-style–calf's liver, floured, butter-fried; served covered with layers of fried onions and fried apples.
>   **Gebraten:** Fried liver.
>   **Ragout "Bombay":** Pieces of liver in a curry sauce.
>   **Scheiben:** Sliced liver.

LEBERKÄS(E): A meat loaf of bacon, beef, pork meat and liver with seasonings. Best served hot with brown gravy. Tastes somewhat like a hotdog. A Bavarian speciality.

LENDEN-: Tenderloin or filet, usually of beef.
>   **Goulasch:** Braised pieces of filet in thick gravy.

LENDEN-: (cont.)

Lendchen: Small pieces of beef tenderloin.

Schnitten: Slices of tenderloin.

Steak: Beef tenderloin, or filet steak.

"Espagnol": Fried, served with glazed onions, rice, stuffed tomatoes, and with sherry seasoned gravy.

"Mirabeau": Grilled tenderloin topped with anchovy filets and surrounded with olives, tarragon leaves.

Natur: Unadorned, simply fried.

"Viktoria": Sauteed, served on chicken croquette, and topped with fried half tomato.

"Westmoreland": Braised in brown tomato sauce with chopped pickles, capers, covered with sliced pickles; or with elaborate mixed vegetable garnish.

MARKKLÖPSCHEN: Beef-marrow dumplings.

MARKKLÖSSE: Same.

MAST: Meaning grain-fed.

MASTOCHSEN-: Fattened steer beef.

Brust: Breast of steer, usually boiled.

Fleisch: Meat of; usually boiled.

Lende: Tenderloin or filet.

Rindfleisch: Fattened beef; usually boiled.

MAULTASCHEN "Schwäb. Art" abgeschmelzt: Flour-dough envelope filled with chopped meat, brains, spinach; i.e., king-size raviolis, served with a sauce.

MEERRETTICH: Horseradish.

MAILÄNDER STEAK: Veal steak breaded, and butter-fried.

MILZWURST: A sausage made of veal spleen.

MÜNCHNER: Munich style.

MÜNSTERLÄNDER: Munster style.

NASI GÖRENG: Seasoned rice with diced pork and beef, sometimes chicken. An Indonesian dish similar to Chinese fried rice, or Indian Pilaf.

NATUR: Unadorned, simply fried.

NIEREN: Kidneys.

NIERCHEN SAUER: Small sliced kidneys braised, and served in a sweet-sour herbal vinegar sauce and sour cream.

NUDELTOPF mit HUHN and SPARGEL: Chicken and noodle casserole with asparagus.

OCHSEN-: Steer beef.

Fleisch gekocht: Boiled beef.

Schwanz-Ragout: Braised ox-tail.

Zunge in Madeira: Ox-tongue served in a Madeira wine sauce.

PANIERTES: Breaded.

PAPRIKAGULASCH: Another expression for Hungarian Goulash.

PAPRIKASCHOTEN, Gefüllte or Gef.: Red, yellow, or green bell peppers stuffed with chopped meat mixture.

"**Ung. Art**": Hungarian style stuffed with herbal rice and ground beef; and cooked in a tomato sauce.

PAPRIKASCHNITZEL: See under Schnitzel.

PFÄLZER: A mild hot dog type sausage from Pfalz area, or can be a small meat loaf.

PFEFFERPOTTHAST: Casserole of cubed beef with peppercorns, spices, onions; sauce thickened with breadcrumbs.

PFEFFERSTEAK: Coarsely ground peppercorns pounded into a steak, then fried.

Flambiert: Flamed with brandy.

PÖKELZUNGE in Madeira: Pickled tongue served hot in Madeira wine sauce.

PRAGER STEAK: Fried veal cutlet or steak, covered with brown gravy, with scrambled eggs, and finely chopped ham on top.

PRESSACK: Pork head-cheese. In Essig und Öl–in vinegar and oil.

PUTENSCHINKEN: Turkey leg.

RAGOUT: A sort of stew; small chunks of meat braised in a brown gravy.

Fin: A rich, finely textured sauce containing diced veal parts, tongue, brains, sweetbreads, mushrooms, herbs, white wine, enriched with egg. Served in a patty shell or any individual shell or container. Can be "au gratin" with grated cheese and breadcrumbs on top put under the broiler.

"**Jäger**": Hunter style–with mushrooms and herbs.

"**Toulouser Art**": Toulouse (France) style–with sliced calf sweetbreads, cocks' combs, kidneys, truffles, mushrooms, in a rich brown sauce.

RAHM-: Another name for cream, or cream-enriched.

Hackbraten: Meat loaf slices in cream-enriched brown gravy.

RATSHERREN: A magistrate's dish–City hall style.

RÄUBERFLEISCH (Bakoyner) am Spieß: "Robber" meat–broiled, corn-fed pork on skewer.

REISFLEISCH: A pilaf–braised meat, cubed, added to rice and cooked in broth until rice is dry, with added seasonings.

REISFLEISCH: (cont.)

    Serbisches: Cubed veal, braised in onions, garlic, tomato puree, paprika; mixed with rice, cooked in broth until rice is dry. Can have also sliced red bell peppers and mushrooms.

REGENSBURGER: A pork, or beef and pork, short, fat, stubby sausage, served boiled or grilled.

REISRAND "Toulouser Art": A rice ring filled with ragout, or a creamy stew of sweetbreads, cocks' combs, kidneys, truffles and mushrooms.

RIND(ER)(S)-: Beef.

    Brust: Shortribs of beef, or beef breast.

    Hacksteak: Ground beef, or hamburger patty.

    Pökelbrust: Pickled beef breast, usually served hot, boiled with sauerkraut.

    Roulade in Burgunder: Rolled thin slices of beef stuffed with bacon, dill pickles, anchovies, capers, onions, and chopped parsley; sauteed in hot fat, and braised in brown stock which is made into a thick gravy.

    Saftbraten: Juicy pot-roast of beef done in abundant liquid and juices.

    Schmorbraten: Beef pot-roast.

    Zunge in Madeira: Fresh, sliced boiled beef tongue in Madeira wine sauce.

        Gepökelt: Pickled beef tongue.

RIPPE: Rib.

RIPPCHEN: Small pork loin chop.

RIPPENBRATEN: Loin pork roast.

ROSENSPITZ: A veal steak, properly for sirloin.

ROST: A grill, either on top of stove, or in oven.

ROSTBRATEN: A cut of beef from loin to sirloin area of beef; could mean a Spencer, Market, Delmonico, T-Bone, Porterhouse or Sirloin steak, without bone. Or can be a roast from this same area.

    "Helgoländer Art": Fried, served on toast; covered with tomato strips, chopped herbs, and Hollandaise sauce.

    "Jäger Art": Beefsteak country-fried with bacon, sliced vegetables, red wine, served in a sauce made of pan juices, pickled cucumbers, onions, capers.

    "Schwäbischer": Usually braised in herbs and vegetables; served in a brown sauce with capers and anchovies, or butter-fried, and served with a cream sauce.

    "Wiener": Vienna style—fried in butter and served covered with fried onions.

ROSTBRATEN: (cont.)

"Zigeuner": Gypsy style–meat seasoned, browned with bacon and onions, braised, or Swiss-fried with cabbage and potatoes added. Covered and cooked until tender.

ROULADE: Rolled stuffed thin cutlets of beef or veal served in a brown gravy. Various garnishes and stuffings determine the cooking style name given to the dish.

Hackroulade: Ground meat in the stuffing of the roulade or beef roll.

RUMPSTEAK: Bottom-round beef steak.

"Mirabeau": Fried, topped with anchovies and sliced olives.

"Provencial": Fried, served with garnish of stuffed or small tomatoes, mushrooms, with tomato sauce flavored with garlic and herbs.

"Rußland": With mushrooms, pickles, onions in brown sauce, or with horseradish.

SAFT-: Juicy–also implying ample sauce or gravy.

Braten: Beef pot-roast done in abundant liquid, to the point that it is juicy.

Goulasch: Juicy goulash; veal stew with paprika, onions, tomato puree, meat stock, served with ample gravy.

SAUERBRATEN: The famous Munich dish. A beef pot-roast marinated several days in vinegar, red wine, carrots, onion, bay leaf, juniper berries, garlic, cloves, salt, water. Browned in hot fat, then pot-roasted with marinade juices, vegetables, paprika, tomato puree, flour.

SAUTIERT: Sauteed.

SCHARFES TÖPFCHEN: Well-seasoned casserole of cubed veal or beef in brown gravy.

SCHASCHLIK "KAUKASISCH": Shish-kebab–marinated chunks of lamb, veal or beef, on skewer, often with alternating pieces of bell pepper, onion, tomato.

SCHASCHLIKSPIESSCHEN: Same as Schaschlik, but indicating on a small skewer.

SCHINKEN: Ham; occasionally means thigh or leg.

Bauern: Farm-cured ham.

Haxe: Ham hocks or shanks.

Katen: Peasant cottage style cured ham.

Knochen: Term applies to Westphalian cured raw ham; bone is in.

Rauch: Smoked.

Rentier: Reindeer meat ham, or leg.

57

SCHINKEN: (cont.)

    Saft: Juicy ham, usually boiled.

    Streifen: Strips of.

SCHLACHTPLATTE: Butcher's plate–a complete meal dish of fresh liver sausage, blood sausage, pork belly, all boiled; served with sauerkraut, potatoes, dumplings.

SCHLACHTSCHÜSSEL: Same as Schlachtplatte.

SCHLEGEL: In veal and pork, the hind leg, upper part.

SCHMORBRATEN: Pot-roast of beef, also means braised.

SCHNITZEL: A cutlet, or boneless, thin veal steak, but when so stated, may be from pork, venison or other meat.

    Holstein(er): Is always a pan-fried veal cutlet served topped with a fried egg, but garnish can include toast triangles with anchovies, smoked salmon, caviar, sardines, plus added pickles, mussels, beets.

    "Hubertus": Butter-fried, served under rich, brown, white wine sauce of shallots, sliced mushrooms.

    "Jäger Art": White wine, tomato sauce with herbs, mushrooms, shallots in dark brown sauce.

    "Mailänder": Milan style modified, floured, dipped in beaten egg, rolled in breadcrumbs and grated Parmesan cheese; butter-fried golden. Served with sauteed sliced mushrooms and tongue. Usually accompanied by brown sauce on spaghetti.

    Natur: Plain, pan-fried veal cutlet.

    Paprika: Paprika-dusted, floured, butter-fried, served with brown sauce with diced bacon, sour cream, lemon juice; topped, half chopped parsley, half paprika-dusted, under slice of lemon.

    Pikantes: Meaning spicy, usually referring to paprika schnitzel, or a sauce.

    Rahm: Butter-fried, then simmered in a lemon juice, sour cream enriched brown sauce.

    Sardellen: Butter-fried; served in rich brown anchovy sauce.

    Schweizer: Swiss–(see "Cordon Bleu").

    Wiener: Vienna style–another renowned dish. A breaded cutlet, butter-fried golden, served topped with lemon slice, or there can also be a rolled anchovy, black olive, chopped capers, sieved egg yolk, chopped egg white, parsley garnish.

    Zigeuner: Gypsy style–more of an Austrian dish which is veal cutlet sauteed in tomato sauce with thin strips of pickled tongue, red bell peppers, mushrooms and possibly truffles. Usually served in a paprikarahm-

SCHNITZEL:

Zigeuner: (cont.)
sauce–a cream-enriched gravy, heavily flavored with paprika.

SCHWÄBISCHE: Swabian style, from Southern Germany.
In schnitzel is cutlet simmered in sour cream sauce and served with spätzle (little, short bumpy noodles).

SCHWEIN(S)(E)-: Pork.

Bauch: Belly-pork which makes bacon. Thick slices boiled.

Braten: Roast; can be leg or shoulder.

Brust: Breast or spareribs.

Füße: Pig's feet.

Haxe: Same as Eisbein–a piece of pork shank cut across lower part of ham. Not feet; and is usually salt-pickled, boiled, served with sauerkraut.

Bürgerlich: Roasted with onions, carrots, meat broth, and flour-thickened sauce.

Gebraten: Fresh pork hock or shank roasted, and served with own pan juices.

Geschmort: Pot-roasted.

Keule: Pork leg (fresh ham): in Bier gedünstet–steamed in beer broth.

Kopfsülze: Pork head-cheese loaf held together with gelatin.

Kotelette: Pork chop, or even cutlet.

Gebacken: Fried; may or may not be breaded.

"Münchner Art": Munich style but could be any of several kinds of braised preparations.

Natur: Plain, fried pork chop.

Paniert: Breaded–dipped in egg, breadcrumbs, and fried golden.

Pfeffer: A highly seasoned pork stew containing pig's blood.

vom **Rost:** Broiled or grilled.

"Ungarisch": Paprika-dusted, fried, and served covered with brown paprika gravy.

"Westmoreland": Fried, smothered with brown sauce and red bell peppers, cauliflower, tiny dill pickles, pearl onions, carrot slices, string beans, tiny asparagus spears.

"Zigeuner Art": Gypsy style–fried, covered with brown sauce having red bell peppers, fried onions, tomatoes, pickle, cayenne pepper, pearl onions.

Leber: Pork liver.

SCHWEIN(S)(E)-:
    Leber: (cont.)
        Sauer: Fried slices in fat with chopped onions, then braised in pan with flour, vinegar, lemon juice, water.
    Lendchen: Pork tenderloin or filet.
    Ungarisch: Sliced, browned in butter; then braised in a light paprika sauce.
    Nacken: Neck and upper back (shoulder, back).
    Niere(n): Kidneys.
    Ohren: Pig's ears.
    Rollbraten: Large piece of pork roast meat, cut flat, rolled, tied, and roasted.
    Rücken: Pork back or loin.
    Schlegel: Leg of pork.
    Schnitzel: Pork cutlet or thin steak.
        Gebraten or Geb.: Fried.
        Paniertes: Breaded, fried golden.
    vom **Rost:** Grilled or broiled.
    mit **Sahnetunke:** Fried, served in a cream-enriched brown stock sauce.
    Schulter: Shoulder of pork.
    Steak: A thin pork steak or cutlet.
    "Metzgerin Art": Butcher's style—buttered, rolled in breadcrumbs and fried.
    Mirabeau: Fried, served covered with strips of anchovies and sliced green olives.
    Wammerl (Gesotten): Pork belly slices, simmered.
SCHWEIZER: Swiss style or origin.
    Schnitzel "Cordon Bleu": (See Cordon Bleu).
SPANFERKEL: Suckling pig.
    Kopferl: Head.
    Leber (Geröstet): Grilled liver of suckling pig.
    am **Spieß:** Spit-roasted suckling pig.
SPECK-: Basically means pork fat, but comes principally from parts that are pickled and then smoked; thus, is our bacon.
    Hackbraten: A meatloaf containing chopped meat and diced smoked bacon.
    Magar: Lean bacon.
    Pfannkuchen: A large diameter, flat, omelette-looking pancake, made of egg, flour and milk with pieces of chopped bacon in it.
    Stippe: Bacon-flavored gravy.
SPIESS: On a skewer, as shish-kebab, or on a spit.

STIPPE: Gravy or sauce.

SULPERKNOCHEN: A stew of pig's ears, tail and feet, served with sauerkraut and mashed peas.

TELLERFLEISCH: Boiled meat of freshly killed pork, or simply boiled beef.

TÖPFCHEN: A casserole dish of veal or beef cubes in brown gravy.

    Scharfes: Sharp, meaning fairly well-seasoned.

    Serbisches: Serbian—with paprika and herbs.

TÖPFCHEN Münsterländer: Calf's head and viscera made into a relatively spicy stew; from Münster.

TOURNEDOS: A French word. Slices from center of beef filet or tenderloin. There are 254 recognized preparations in Germany.

    Chateleine: Sauteed and served on stuffed artichoke bottoms in a Madeira wine sauce with glazed chestnuts and nut-sized potatoes as garnish.

    Rossini: Fried, served on toast topped with sauteed round of goose fois gras (liver) and slice of truffle, covered with Madeira wine sauce, containing truffle essence.

TUNKE: Sauce or gravy.

UNGARISCHES: Hungarian; their dishes very popular.

VOM: From.

WAMMERL (Hausger.): House-smoked pork belly (bacon).

VELLFLEISCH: Boiled, fresh-killed pork meat.

VESTFÄLISCHER: Westphalian—the famous ham area.

VIENER: From Vienna, or Viennese style.

    Goulasch: A stew of cubed beef braised in onions, pork fat, with paprika, vinegar, garlic and herbs.

    Rahmbeuscherl: Calf's lung, pre-cooked, cut in strips, braised in rich white cream sauce with anchovies, rosemary, parsley, lemon peel and capers.

    Rahmschlegel: Leg of pork with a cream sauce.

    Schnitzel: (See under Schnitzel).

    Würstchen: Small Vienna style hot dogs, usually boiled.

    Zwiebelrostbraten: Fried beef loin steak served topped with fried onions.

WURST: Sausage.

WÜRZFLEISCH: Beef chunks of round steak stewed, or braised in, and served with a spiced brown sauce.

IGEUNER-: Gypsy style—a term much used.

    Rostbraten: Spiced ribsteak browned with little squares of bacon, sliced cabbage, potatoes, then braised.

ZIGEUNER-: (cont.)

Schnitzel: (See under Schnitzel.)

Spieß: Broiled slices of pork tenderloin with bacon and vegetables for garnish; on a skewer.

Steak: Beef or veal steak pan-fried, covered with mushrooms, red or green bell peppers, onions, pickles, chopped ham, in a brown sauce.

ZUNGE(N)-: Tongue.

Ragout "Marengo": Braised in olive oil with tomatoes, garlic, white wine; served with a garnish of button mushrooms, pearl onions, fried croutons.

Streifen: Strips of tongue.

ZÜNGERL (Gebacknes): Fried small tongues.

ZWIEBEL(N)-: Onions.

Fleisch Münchner: A Munich dish; thin, lean beef slices sauteed in fried onions, then braised with onions in a gravy made by adding flour and bouillon to meat juices. Actually, same as Swiss-fried or country-fried or chicken-fried.

Rostbraten: Loin or club steak prepared same way but may be only fried, then served topped with fried onions.

ZWISCHENRIPPENSTÜCK: A beef loin steak, that is, a boneless T-bone steak.

GEFLÜGEL und WILD
(Fowl and Game)

The domestic fowl, and the wild fowl, and the four-footed wild game are customarily combined in the same category on the menu, except on the daily menu (TAGES-KARTE), where they are among the meat dishes.

Venison is offered throughout the year, and wild fowl in autumn and winter. It can be said that game abounds, and the reason for this is that it is a crop which is harvested under very strict regulations and supervision. The professional JÄGER (hunter) knows the name, and serial number of each deer and wild pig in his area, and the taking of the animals is carefully controlled. The wild fowl, pheasant, partridge and others, are sold from estate shooting, and Jäger controlled shooting.

The usual venison is REH (roebuck, a specie of small deer), HIRSCH (antlered deer) and DAM (the fallow deer). The wild birds include FASAN (pheasant), REBHUHN (partridge), WILDENTE (wild duck), SCHNEPPE (woodcock), WILDTAUBE (wild pigeon), WACHTEL (quail), and others.

Both the wild birds and the domestic such as TAUBE (pigeon), HUHN or GEFLÜGEL (chicken), ENTE (duck), GANS (goose), PUTER or TRUTHAHN (turkey), and PERLHUHN (guinea fowl), are cooked in the traditional methods such as stuffed and roasted, grilled, fried, fricasseed, stewed, or in casserole.

The animal game is frequently marinated prior to cooking, and is accompanied by various sugar-preserved fruits such as PFIRSICHE (peaches), PFLAUMEN (plums), ANANAS (pineapple), KIRSCHEN (cherries), BIRNE (pears), PREISELBEEREN or KRONSBEEREN (types of cranberries), JOHANNISBEEREN (red currants), as a garnish. Sliced PILZE (mushrooms), as well as PAPRIKASCHOTEN (bell peppers) are often included in the gravy.

BACKHENDL: Austrian name for Backhuhn (see below).

BACKHUHN: Fried chicken, usually disjointed, breaded and deep-fried, unless other "ART" (style) is indicated.

BAUERN-ENTE: Farm-grown duck.

BRATHÄHNCHEN or BRATHUHN: Large fryer chicken, roasted, or spit-roasted, fried, sauteed, or cooked in casserole.

BRATHENDL: Austrian name for Brathuhn (see above).

CURRYHUHN: Curried chicken (fricasseed chicken in curry sauce).

DAM: A specie of deer, the fallow deer.

DAMWILDKEULE: Leg of fallow deer.

ELCH: Elk.

ENTE: Duck.

FASAN: Pheasant.

FASAN im TOPF: Pheasant, roasted whole in butter in a covered pot or casserole.

FASANHUHN: Hen pheasant.

FÖRSTERTOPF mit **PILZEN:** Casserole of venison with mushrooms.

FRIKASSEE: Strictly speaking, a dish, or a ragout (a kind of stew), in which the meat has been seared or browned (in the case of chicken or white meat, merely cooked until meat has swollen and stiffened), then floured and final cooking done in stock. Sauce develops in the cooking.

FRIKASSEE vom HUHN: Fricasseed chicken.

GANS: Goose.

GANSBRATEN: Roast goose.

GÄNSEBRUST: Breast of goose, special delicacy when smoked.

GEDÄMPFTER, as in REHSCHLEGEL: Braised, i.e., browned in fat to which water is added for the cooking. In this case leg of venison (ROEBUCK).

GEFLÜGEL-: Poultry, i.e., chickens principally, but in general, a term for birds.

    Klein: Chicken giblets.

    Leber: Chicken livers.

    Ragout: Usually means chicken stew, as fricasseed chicken.

    Reisbombe: Pilaf (as chicken fried rice) served in a round mold.

    Risotto: Milanese rice pilaf, pieces of cooked chicken in saffron, herbal rice.

GEFÜLLTE: Stuffed.

GERÄUCHERTE: Smoked.

GESCHNETZELTE HÄHNCHENBRUST: Small pieces of tender chicken breasts cooked in a rich cream sauce.

HÄHNCHEN-: Small frying chicken.

    Mägen: Chicken giblets.

HASE: Hare, a specie of large-sized rabbit, as our jack rabbit.

HASENKEULE: Leg or thigh of hare.

HASENPFEFFER: Pieces of marinated hare browned in hot fat then cooked in a roux to which is added red wine, herbs, onions, mushrooms, blood of the hare, and the marinating liquid to make the sauce. This hare stew is a renowned German dish.

HIRSCH-: A specie of very large (up to 600 lbs.) antlered deer.

> **Kalb:** A calf, or hirsch faun.
>
> **Keule:** A leg of venison (of hirsch).
>
> **Ragout:** Venison stew (of hirsch).

HUHN (HÜHNER)-: Chicken, but means fowl, and can include game birds.

> **Brust (Brüstchen)-:** Breast of chicken, de-boned; strictly speaking, the filet, or section lying near to the breast bone.
>
> **Frikassee:** Chicken fricassee.
>
> **Ragout:** Stew, or fricassee of chicken.

JÄGER: Hunter.

JÄGERSPIESS: Skewered meat, probably venison, broiled or sauteed in a sauce.

JUNGE(R): Young.

KAPAUN: Capon.

KLEIN: Giblets as Ganseklein, goose giblets.

MAST-: Prefix meaning grain-fed or fattened.

> **Ente:** Fattened duck.
>
> **Gansbraten:** Roasted grain-fed goose.
>
> **Hähnchen:** Small grain-fed chicken fryer.
>
> **Huhn:** Fattened roasting chicken.
>
> **Poularde:** Fattened roasting chicken.
>
> **Puter:** Fattened turkey.

PAPRIKAHÄHNCHEN "UNGARISCH": Chicken braised in a paprika sauce with sour cream and tomato paste.

PAPRIKASAHNEHUHN: Chicken served in a paprika cream sauce.

PERLHUHN: Guinea fowl.

PILZE: Variety of wild mushroom.

POULARDE: Grain-fed roasting chicken.

PUTER-: Turkey.

> **Braten:** Roast turkey.
>
> **Schinken:** Turkey leg (not ham).

RAGOUT: A generic term for dishes which appear to us to be a stew—uniformly cut pieces of meat and vegetablies in a thick, rich white or brown sauce. Can be the main dish, or a garnishing stew or sauce for other dishes, or a filling for rice-rings, patty shells, etc.

REBHUHN: Partridge.

REH-: Venison from the Roebuck, a specie of small deer.

    Braten: Roast venison.

    Keule: Leg or thigh of venison.

    Medallions: Small round thick slices or discs of loin or tenderloin of venison.

    Ragout: Rich stew of cubes of venison and other ingredients.

    Rücken: Saddle or back of venison.

    "Jägermeister": Saddle of venison roasted and served in a sauce which includes shallots, mushrooms white wine.

    "Baden-Baden": Marinated saddle of venison baked in the oven, and served with a thick brown sauce and a garnish of pears cooked in cinnamon-flavored syrup and red currant jelly.

    Schauferl: Shoulder of venison.

    Schlegel: Leg of venison.

    Schnitzel: Boneless cutlet of venison.

RENTIER: Reindeer.

RENTIERSCHINKEN: Ham made of leg of reindeer, o just the leg itself.

SCHNEPFE: Woodcock.

STUBENKÜKEN: Very young broiler chicken.

SUPREM(E) vom MASTHUHN: Boned breast of chicke (the supreme), served in many different sauces.

TAUBE: Pigeon.

TOULOUSER GEFLÜGEL-PASTETE: A ragout or chicken la king with mushrooms and truffle slices in a patty shel

TRUTHAHN: Turkey.

WACHTEL: Quail.

WIENER BACKHUHN: Fried chicken, Vienna style, quarte ed, breaded, deep-fried, garnished with fried parsley.

WILD: Meaning game in general.

WILDENTE: Wild duck.

WILDRÜCKENSTEAK: Venison steak from loin or saddle.

WILDSCHWEIN-: A wild pig, what we call wild boar—i either boar or sow.

    Braten: Roast wild boar.

    Ragout: Wild boar stew.

    Schinken: Ham made from wild boar, normally leg o

    Schnitzel: Wild boar cutlet (no bone).

WILDSTEAK: Usually venison steak.

WILDTAUBEN: Wild pigeon.

MIT
(With)

This section translates all the vegetables, starches, fruits, garnishes, condiments and sauces which come with the main dishes. It also lists the terms and expressions which you will encounter in connection with these accompaniments.

MIT: This means WITH. First, the meat and its preparation are listed in the main course dishes. But, the meat course is served with some combination of vegetables, starches, sauces, condiments, fruits. How to devise a RAPID system to translate and identify these seemingly infinite combinations of garnishes?

Since the meat dishes are served MIT these variables, let us have a section called "MIT", wherein we list them alphabetically together with the expressions you will find connected with them. Thus, first you identify the meat being offered; then you turn to the "MIT" section to translate all the various things served with that dish.

The following are the other categories of the menu also covered in this section:

BEILAGEN: Supplemental dishes, vegetables, salads.

GEMÜSE und BEILAGEN: Vegetables and other supplemental dishes.

GEMÜSE: Vegetables.

GEMÜSE und SALATE: Vegetables and salads (not the ones dressed with mayonnaise).

GEMÜSE und BEILAGEN
(Vegetables and Other Supplemental Dishes)

Most vegetables familiar to Americans are also eaten in Germany, but they are not given much significance, for the meat and the starch are the important parts of every entree, with the vegetables, if any, usually serving as a garnish. In general, very few fresh vegetables are offered with a meat course, but you will often encounter canned ones.

An exception is SPARGEL (asparagus), in season, widely offered fresh, and they can also constitute a main course. This is also true of certain other vegetables such as BLUMENKOHL (cauliflower), which when combined with ham and a sauce would make a main course, as would GEFÜLLTE AUBERGINE or EIERPFLANZE (meat-

67

stuffed eggplant), or GEFÜLLTE PAPRIKASCHOTEN (stuffed bell peppers).

ROTKOHL (cooked red cabbage) or WEISSKOHL (white cabbage), flavored with diced ham or bacon, apples, or other fruit are common preparations, but most of the cabbage is converted into sauerkraut.

KARTOFFELN (potatoes), perhaps THE staple starch, are cooked in a seemingly endless variety of ways, and are often served with sauerkraut, and possibly another starch, such as noodles or dumplings to accompany a meat dish. In the listing, all methods of preparing potatoes are under the heading of KARTOFFELN (potatoes), even though the way in which they are cooked may be a prefix attached to the main word as in DAMPFKARTOFFELN (boiled or steamed).

PAPRIKASCHOTEN (Bell peppers) and PILZEN (mushrooms) both wild and cultivated, are used extensively in game dishes, and these along with GEWÜRZGURKE, PERLZWIEBELN, KAPERN (pickles, pearl onions, and capers) are added to sauces and gravies.

You will find certain delicate vegetables, but canned, such as PALMENMARK (palm hearts), ARTISCHOCKEN-BÖDEN or -HERZEN (artichoke bottoms or hearts), and SPARGELSPITZEN (asparagus tips).

SALATEN (salads) are very small when served as accompaniment to an entree or light hot dish. They will be TOMATEN (sliced tomatoes), GURKEN (cucumbers), SELLERIE (celery root), ROTE RÜBEN (cooked beets), BOHNEN (cooked green beans), or various kinds of KOPFSALAT (lettuce), all mixed with a vinegar based, watery, cream salad dressing.

Salads served as VORSPEISEN (appetizers) are the ones of meat, fish, vegetables, or combinations of all these mixed with a heavy, rich thick mayonnaise or sour cream dressing. The traditional German KARTOFFELSALAT (potato salad) is normally served with hot WÜRSTCHEN (sausages).

Various words are used for sauce: SAUCE, TUNKE, SOSSE, SUD, STIPPE, and they use three different words for cream: CREME, SAHNE, RAHM: and a sauce labeled a cream sauce may or may not have cream in it, for this implies creamy in texture.

MIT
(With)

ABGEBRÄUNT: Browned quickly, or grilled.

ABGESCHMECKT: Taste-tested.

ABGESCHMELZT: Melted, or to put over or on top of, as pouring sauce over vegetables.

ALLERLEI: All sorts of.

AM: On.

ANGEMACHT: Ready to serve, pre-prepared, or made with.

ANANAS: Pineapple.

ANANASKRAUT: Sauerkraut with pineapple.

APFEL: Apple.

APFELBLAUKRAUT: Red cabbage cooked with apples.

APFELMUS: Applesauce.

APFELRINGE: Apple rings.

APFELROTKOHL: Red cabbage cooked with apples.

APFELROTKRAUT: The same.

APFELSCHEIBEN: Slices of apple.

APRIKOSEN: Apricots.

ARTISCHOCKENBÖDEN: Artichoke bottoms, usually canned.

ARTISCHOCKENHERZEN: Artichoke hearts, usually canned.

AUBERGINE: Eggplant.

AUF: On, as on toast.

AUFSCHNITT: Cold cuts.

AUS: From.

BACKOBST: Dried fruit boiled to make a compote, or stewed fruit.

BACKPFLAUME: Prune.

BAMBUSSPROSSEN: Bamboo sprouts (canned).

BANANE: Bananas.

BASILIKUM: Basil, the herb.

BAUERNBROT: Peasant bread, a dark-crusted, heavy, greyish bread.

BEETE: A spelling for beets.

BEILAGE(N): A garnish, or an accompaniment; supplemental vegetables, additions.

BELEGT: Covered with.

BERCY: The rich creamy French sauce of butter, shallots, white wine, stock, beef marrow, parsley.

BERNAISE: The thick French sauce of butter and egg yolks, slowly cooked with herb-flavored vinegar.

BETE: Beet.

69

BIRNE: Pear.

BLATTSPINAT: Leaf spinach.

BLAU: "Blue"—may refer to live fish, usually taken from the fish tank in the restaurant, and boiled.

BLUMENKOHL: Cauliflower.

BOHNEN: Beans, usually modified to tell what type, as green, string, white.

BOHNENSALAT: String bean salad, or bean salad.

BORDELAISE: The French sauce of red wine, beef marrow, cooking juices, chopped shallots, and herbs.

BRAUNE BUTTER: Browned butter.

BRAUNKOHL: Another name for GRÜNKOHL–kale.

BRECHBOHNEN: String beans broken into lengths.

BROKKOLI: Broccoli.

BRÖTCHEN: A roll, usually a white bread roll.

BRUNNENKRESSE: Watercress.

BÜCHSENSTANGENSPARGEL: Canned asparagus spears (white).

BUNTER SALATTELLER: Mixed salad plate.

BURGUNDER WEINSAUCE: Burgundy wine sauce.

BUTTERBOHNEN or ERBSEN, or KAROTTEN: Buttered string beans, peas, carrots.

BUTTERNUDELN: Buttered noodles.

BUTTERREIS: Buttered rice.

CHAMPIGNON(S): Mushrooms, the cultivated variety.

> **Rahmsauce:** Mushroom cream sauce.
>
> **Tunke:** Mushroom sauce.

CHEN: A diminutive suffex; little ones.

CHICOREE: Chicory, but means Belgian endive, small, narrow, greenish-yellow crisp-leafed head, used as a salad green or cooked vegetable.

CONFITÜRE: Jam, the French word for it.

CREMESAUCE: Cream sauce.

DAMPFNUDELN: Flour dumplings with yeast dough.

DAZU: In addition (to).

DICKE: Thick (as a slice), wide.

DICKE BOHNEN: Broad or horse beans.

DIENST: Service.

DILL-: Dill, or dillweed.

> **Rahmsauce:** Dill-flavored cream sauce.
>
> **Tunke:** Dill sauce.

DIVERSEN (or DIV.): Various, several, mixed.

DOPPELTES: Double, usually of size or portion.

DOSE: A can of, as a can of sardines; a portion.

ECHTE: Real, genuine.

EDEL: Noble, or fine, or excellent.

EDELPILZEN: Mushrooms (fine quality).

EI(ER)-: Eggs.

    Einlauf: With egg in it.

    Kuchen: Egg pancakes.

    Pfannkuchen: Egg pancakes.

    Spätzle: Short, bumpy, thick egg noodles.

    Teigwaren: Egg noodles.

EIHÜLLE: Egg-covered, or dipped in egg batter.

EINGELEGTE(R): Pickled.

EINGEMACHT: Preserved, or tinned, or canned.

EINLAGE: Something included in.

ENDIVIEN: Endive, or chicory, the crinkly-leafed lettuce-like salad head.

ERBSBREI: Puree of green peas, usually dried ones.

ERBSEN: Peas.

ERBSPÜREE: Pureed peas.

ERDBIRNEN: Jerusalem artichokes, a tuber, like a long thin parsnip, with a delicate flavor.

ERLESENE: First class or choice.

ESSIG: Vinegar.

ESSIGGURKEN: Pickles, vinegar-pickled.

FARBSTOFF: Artificial coloring.

FARCE: Stuffing.

FEIN(ER)(ES): Delicate or fine in texture or quality.

FEINEM RAGOUT: See under meat section.

FENCHEL: Fennel, the licorice-tasting, celery-like vegetable.

FERTIGE: Ready-cooked; ready to eat.

FLAMBIERT(E): Flamed; brandy poured over, and then ignited.

FLEISCHKLÖSSCHEN: Small meat-bread dumplings.

FLUSS: River, or stream.

FLÜSSIGER (SAHNE): Thick cream.

FÖRSTER: Forester, gamekeeper.

FRISCHE(M)(R), or FR.: Fresh.

FRÜCHT(EN): Fruit.

FÜLLUNG: Filling.

GÄNSESCHMALZ: Goose fat or grease, used as butter.

GANZ(E): Complete, whole, entire.

GARNIERT(E): Garnished.

GE: The past participle designator for verbs.

GEBÄCK: Cookies, wafers, small pastries–baked goods.

GEBACKEN or GEB.: Can mean fried or deep-fried, or baked.

MIT

71

GEBACKENES: Baked goods.

GEBEIZTER: Pickled.

GEBRATEN(E) or GEB.: Means fried, principally, but can also mean roasted, or even braised; has a general sense of meaning cooked.

GEBUNDENE(R): Flour-thickened, as in soup or sauce.

GEDÄMPFT(EN)(ER): Steamed.

GEDECK: Cover, as in table cover, or a fixed price meal.

GEDÜNSTET(E)(EN)(ER): Braised, steamed, stewed, simmered.

GEFÜLLT(E)(ES) or GEF.: Stuffed.

GEKOCHTE(R)(M)(N): Boiled.

GEMÜSE: Vegetables.

> **Beilage:** Accompaniment or garnish.
>
> **Platte:** Vegetable plate.
>
> **Salat:** Vegetable salad.

GEPÖKELT: Pickled, salt or salt-brine cured.

GERÄUCHERT(EM): Smoked.

GERIEBENE(R)(N)(M): Ground or grated, as with horseradish.

GERÖSTET(EN): Roasted.

GESCHMORT(E): Pot-roasted, cooked covered.

GESCHABTES: Scraped, minced, or ground.

GESOTTEN: Simmered, boiled.

GEWÜRZ(E)(T): Spices, spiced.

GEWÜRZGURKE: Pickle.

GLAS: Glass.

GLASIERT(E): Glazed, as ham or carrots.

GRIESSKLÖSSEN: Semolina flour dumplings.

GRILL (vom): Grilled.

GROSS(E)(ER): Large.

GRÜN(E)(ER): Green.

> **Bohnen:** Green beans, string beans.
>
> **Salat:** Green salad.
>
> **Kohl:** Kale, dark green leaf vegetable similar to mustard greens or Swiss chard, but with curly crinkly leaves.

GURKEN: Cucumber.

GURKENSALAT: Cucumber salad.

HACK: Ground, chopped, or minced.

HACKPETER: Chopped parsley, abbreviation for.

HAPPEN: A morsel, or a snack.

HARTGEKOCHT(E)(N): Hard-boiled, as an egg.

HAUSGEMACHTE(R)(N), or HAUSGEM.: House or home-made.

72

HAUSGEPÖKELT(E)(ES): Home-pickled; home-cured.

HAUSGERÄUCHERTES or HAUSGER.: House or home-style smoked.

HAUSMACHER: Homemade.

HIESIG(ER): Native or local.

HEISS: Hot.

HOLLANDAISE SAUCE: The French sauce of egg yolks and butter cooked together and flavored with lemon juice. Thick and creamy.

HOLZBRETT: A wooden plank.

HOLZTELLER: A wooden dish or plate.

HÜLSENFRÜCHTE: Legumes; vegetables which come in a pod, as peas.

IM: In.

INGWER: Ginger.

INGWERSAHNE: Ginger cream (sauce).

JUNG(E)(N)(R), or JG.: Young, fresh, tender.

KAISER: Implies fine quality, or large size, or both.

KAISERSCHOTEN: Small peas.

KALT(ER): Cold.

KAPERN: Capers.

KAROTTEN: Carrots.

KAROTTENGEMÜSE: Carrots.

KARTOFFELN: Potatoes. Below are some of the different preparations you will find on menus:

> **Bratkartoffeln:** Sliced boiled potatoes, pan-fried.
>
> **Brühkartoffeln:** Boiled in broth; can be cubed with diced vegetables added.
>
> **Dampfkartoffeln:** Boiled or steamed.
>
> **Gebackene Kartoffeln:** Baked potatoes.
>
> **Geröstete Kartoffeln:** Sliced, boiled potatoes, pan-fried.
>
> **Herzoginkartoffeln:** Duchess; mashed potatoes put through a pastry tube into various shapes, and browned in oven or pan-fried.
>
> **Kartoffelbällchen:** Mashed potatoes formed into little balls, and pan-fried.
>
> **Kartoffelbrei:** Pureed, mashed.
>
> **Kartoffelchips:** Potato chips.
>
> **Kartoffelklöße:** Potato dumplings.
>
> **Kartoffelknödel:** Potato dumplings.
>
> **Kartoffeln "Kronprinzessin Art":** Dauphine; mashed, mixed with pastry dough, formed, breaded, and deep-fried.
>
> **Kartoffelkrusten:** Pan-fried until crispy.

KARTOFFELN: (cont.)

Kartoffeln Lyonnaise: Sliced boiled potatoes, fried in lard, and served with added fried onions.

Kartoffelmus: Pureed or mashed.

Kartoffelpuffer: Potato pancakes.

Kartoffelpüree: Mashed or pureed.

Kartoffelkroketten: Potato croquettes.

Lyoner Kartoffeln: Sliced boiled potatoes, fried in lard, and served with added fried onions.

Neue Kartoffeln: New potatoes.

Nußkartoffeln: Nut-shaped raw potatoes, parboiled, browned in butter in a frying pan.

Pellkartoffeln: Potatoes boiled in their jackets (with the skin on).

Petersilienkartoffeln: Boiled, served with chopped parsley on top.

Pommes Frites: French fried potatoes.

Röstkartoffeln: Raw, cooked in hot butter in oven or in pan on stove.

Risoleekartoffeln: Slivered boiled potatoes, sauteed in butter.

Sahnepüreekartoffeln: Mashed, with cream added.

Salzkartoffeln: Boiled in salted water.

Schloßkartoffeln: Potatoes cut in small oval shape and fried in butter.

Schneekartoffeln: Boiled, then riced; nothing added.

Schwenkkartoffeln: Boiled potatoes fried in butter or lard.

Schmelzkartoffeln: Egg-shaped, raw; cooked slowly in covered pan.

Speckkartoffeln: Fried (pan) with bits of bacon.

Strohkartoffeln: Matchstick potatoes.

Würfelkartoffeln: Diced potatoes, fried.

KARTOFFELSALAT: This is the famous German potato salad. Can be either hot or cold. Hot: sauteed onions and bacon with vinegar and meat stock are poured over sliced boiled potatoes. Cold: vinegar and meat stock are poured over cold sliced boiled potatoes and chopped onions. Then salad oil is folded in. May have other cooked vegetables or herbs mixed in and may also be dressed with mayonnaise.

KÄSE: Cheese.

KLEIN(E)(EN): Little, small.

KLÖSSE(N): Dough, or meat and dough dumplings.

KLÖSSCHEN: Small dumplings as above.

KNÖDEL: A dumpling or meatball, with bread in it.

KNUSPRIGE: Crisp or crackling.

KOCHEN: Boiled.

KOHL: Cabbage.

KOHLRABI: Kohlrabi, a turnip-sized, green skinned vegetable which tastes, raw, like a cabbage heart.

KOHLRÄBCHENGEMÜSE: Kohlrabi.

KONFITÜRE: Jam.

KOPFSALAT: Lettuce salad.

KNOBLAUCH: Garlic.

KRÄUTER(N): Herbs.

KRAUT: Can mean herb, vegetables, plant, or cabbage.

KRÄUTERBUTTER: The French ''a la Maitre d'Hotel''; is butter creamed with chopped parsley, white pepper, and lemon juice. Can also include other green herbs.

KRAUTSALAT: Coleslaw.

LAND: Local, country.

LATTICH: Lettuce.

LAUCH: Leeks.

LEBERKNÖDEL: Liver dumplings (see Meat section).

LEBERSPÄTZLE: Small, short, stubby, thick liver noodles.

LECKERBISSEN: A dainty morsel, a tidbit.

MAGER: Lean, as lean bacon.

MANDELN: Almonds.

MANDELKROKETTEN: Almond croquettes of potatoes and almonds.

MANDELSPLITTER: Almond chips.

MANGOLD: Swiss chard.

MARINIERTER: Marinated.

MARKSAUCE: A rich sauce with beef bone marrow in it.

MARMELADE: Jam.

MEERRETTICH: Horseradish.

MEHL: Flour.

MIRABELLEN: Small yellow plums.

MISCHGEMÜSE: Mixed vegetables.

MISCHPILZE: Mixed mushrooms.

MÖHREN: Carrots.

MOHRRÜBE: Carrots.

MORCHELN: Morel mushrooms, a wild variety.

NACH: After the style of, or according to as NACH WAHL, of your choice.

NACH JAHRESZEIT: In season.

NATUR: Natural, plain, unadorned.

NEUE(N): New.

NOCKERLN: Dumplings.

MIT

NUDELN: Noodles, including factory-made ones, as vermicelli.

NUSS: Nut.

OBSTSALAT: Fruit salad.

ODER or OD.: Or.

OHNE: Without.

ÖL: Oil.

OLIVE: Olive.

ORANGENFILETS: Orange sections.

PANIERT(ES): Breaded and fried in a pan, not deep-fried.

PAPRIKARAHMSAUCE: Cream sauce flavored with paprika.

PAPRIKASCHOTEN: Green, yellow, or red bell peppers.

PERLZWIEBELN: Pearl onions.

PETERSILIE: Parsley.

PFANNKUCHEN: Pan-fried; large diameter pancake, heavy with eggs, looking like an unrolled, flat omelette.

PFEFFER: Pepper.

PFIFFERLINGE: Mushrooms, a wild variety.

PFIRSICHE: Peach.

PFLAUMEN: Plums.

PIKANTE(S)(N): Spicy, with possibly a touch of hotness.

PILZEN: Mushrooms.

PLATTE: A plate, or a dish.

POMMES FRITES or POM. FR., or **FRIT.:** French fried potatoes.

PREISSELBEEREN: A small red berry very similiar to the U.S. cranberry.

PÜREESOCKEL: A bed of puree, as a bed of mashed potatoes.

PRINZESSBOHNEN: Long thick, French string beans.

RADIESCHEN: Radishes.

RAHM: Cream.

RAHMSPINAT: Creamed spinach.

REICHLICH: Ample, copious, abundant.

REIS: Rice.

REISRAND: Rice ring; a ring of rice from a mold; then usually filled with a mixture including the sauce.

RETTICH: Radish.

RETTICHSALAT: Radish salad.

RIESE(N): Enormous, gigantic, king-size.

RÖGGELCHEN: Rye roll.

ROH: Raw.

ROHKOSTSALAT: Raw vegetable salad.

RÖHRE: Oven.

ROSENKOHL: Brussel sprouts.

ROSINEN: Raisins.

ROSMARIN: Rosemary, the herb.

ROST: A grill, either in the oven or on top of the stove.

RÖSTZWIEBELN: Onions fried crisp.

ROTE BETE: Red beets.

ROTE RÜBEN: Red beets.

ROTWEINSOSSE: Red wine sauce.

RÜBE: Turnips.

RÜHREI: Fried egg.

SAFT: Juice or juicy.

SAFRAN: Saffron.

SAHNE: Cream.

SAHNEMEERRETTICH: Horseradish cream sauce.

SAHNEPÜREE: Mashed potatoes with cream added.

SALBEI: Sage.

SALAT-: Salad, or lettuce. Can be anything from a simple tossed green one to a heavy mayonnaise-laced one with pickles, apples, onions, meat, chicken or fish.

    Beilage: Salad garnish or accompaniment.

    Mimosa: Lettuce salad with sieved hard-boiled egg yolk over it.

    Platte: Mixed salad plate.

    Teller: Mixed salad plate.

SALZ: Salt.

SAUCE or SC.: Sauce or gravy.

SAUER: Sour, or pickled, or marinated.

SAUERKRAUT: Sauerkraut; shredded, fermented salt-cured cabbage; boiled in wine, water, stock, beer, or other liquid.

SAUERRAHM: Sour cream.

SAUTIERT(E): Sauteed; quickly browned or fried over high heat.

SCHALOTTEN: Shallots.

SCHARF: Sharp, spicy, or bitey, or vinegary.

SCHEIBE(N): Slice, as slice of bread.

SCHINKENFARCE: Chopped ham stuffing.

SCHLEMMER: Gourmet.

SCHMINKBOHNEN: Kidney beans.

SCHMORBRATEN: Braised, or pot-roasted.

SCHNITTE(N): A slice, or a piece, or a dish of, as well as meaning cold cuts or a snack.

SCHNITTLAUCH: Chives.

SCHNITTLAUCHSAUCE or SC.: Cream sauce with chopped chives in it.

SCHOTE: Pod, husk, or shell.

SCHOTENSALAT: Bell pepper salad.

SCHWARZ: Black or dark.

SCHWARZWURZELN: Salsify.

SELLERIE: Celery root.

SELLERIESALAT: Celery root salad.

SEMMELKLÖSSE: Bread, or meat and bread dumplings.

SEMMELKNÖDEL: Bread, or meat and bread dumplings.

SENF: Mustard.

SENFBUTTER: Mustard flavored butter.

SENFGURKEN: Mustard pickles, or cucumbers pickled with mustard seeds included.

SERVIETTENKNÖDEL: Literally, a napkin dumpling. It is a huge bread dumpling cooked in a napkin to hold it together, flavored with onion and parsley. A portion is served covered with butter or meat and a sauce.

SETZEI: Fried egg.

SOCKEL (REIS): A base, as a bed of rice.

SOSSE: Sauce or gravy.

SPARGEL: Asparagus, usually white.

SPARGELKOHL: Broccoli.

SPARGELSALAT: Asparagus salad, most likely canned cold with oil and vinegar.

SPÄTZLE: Small, short, stubby, bumpy, thick noodles.

SPECK-: Bacon.

> **Bohnen:** String beans (or dried ones) cooked with diced bacon.
>
> **Kraut:** Cabbage cooked with bacon.
>
> **Krautsalat:** Cabbage salad flavored with bacon.
>
> **Pfifferlinge:** Mushrooms sauteed with bacon.
>
> **Pilze(n):** The same, but a different variety of wild mushroom.
>
> **Sauce or Sc.:** Bacon flavored sauce or gravy.
>
> **Stippe:** The same; another name for sauce.

SPIESS: Skewer or spit.

SPIEGELEIER(N): Fried eggs (mirror eggs).

SPINAT: Spinach.

STANGENBOHNEN: Green string or pole beans.

STANGENSELLERIE: Stalk celery.

STANGENSPARGEL: Asparagus spears.

STAUDENSELLERIE: Stalk celery.

STECKRÜBE: Turnips.

STEINPILZE(N): A variety of wild mushroom; yellow Boletus.

STIPPE: Sauce or gravy.

STREICH: Spreadable (soft), as in butter.

78

STREIFEN: Strips.

STÜCK: A piece or a portion.

SUCCINI: Zucchini squash.

SÜLZE: In aspic, encased in gelatin.

TAFEL: Table quality or select.

TAFELPILZE: Select mushrooms.

TARTARSAUCE: Tartar sauce—a mayonnaise with chopped pickles, onions, perhaps capers.

TEIGWAREN: Dishes of starch foods, such as spaghetti, macaroni, noodles.

TOAST: Toast.

TOMATEN-: Tomatoes.

> **Salat:** Tomato salad.
>
> **Würfel:** Diced or cubed.

TRAUBEN: Grapes.

TRÜFFEL(N): Truffles.

TUNKE: Another name for sauce or gravy.

ÜBER-: Over.

> **Backen:** Cooked under broiler in the oven.
>
> **Glänzt:** Glazed on top, or glistening.
>
> **Zogen:** Coated or basted.

UMLEGT: Around, or surrounded by (as a garnish around or surrounding a dish).

UMZINGELT: Surrounded (ing).

UNSERE: Our.

WACHOLDER: Juniper berries.

WACHOLDERRAHM: Juniper berry cream sauce.

WACHSBOHNEN: Wax beans.

WAHL: Choice, as NACH WAHL, of your choice.

WALDPILZE(N): Forest mushrooms.

WASSER: Water.

WEICH: Soft, as in soft-boiled egg.

WEINKRAUT: Cabbage or sauerkraut cooked in white wine; may have apples also.

WEINSAUERKRAUT: Same as above.

WEISS(E)(R): White.

> **Bohnen:** White beans, dried.
>
> **Kohl:** White cabbage; just plain cabbage.
>
> **Kraut:** White cabbage.
>
> **Wein:** White wine.

WIRSINGGEMÜSE: Savoy cabbage, the crinkly-leafed variety.

WIRSINGKOHL: Same as above.

WÜRFEL: Cubed or diced.

WURZEL: Root vegetable, as carrots, beets.

MIT

WÜRZE: Spice, seasoning, pickled.

ZART(ES): Tender, mild, or mildly, as smoked, or soft, delicate.

ZERLASSENER: Melted, as in butter.

ZITRONE: Lemon.

ZUBEREITET: Ready to serve; pre-prepared, or prepared at the table, or made with.

ZUCKER: Sugar.

ZUCKERERBSEN: Sweet green peas.

ZWEI: Two.

ZWIEBEL(N)-: Onions.

> **Ringen:** Onion rings, usually with a batter, and deep-fried.

SÜSS-SPEISEN
(Desserts)

This section translates the desserts, ice creams, fruits, which dishes you will find listed under any of the following expressions:

EIS: Ice creams.
EISSPEZIALITÄTEN: Ice cream specialities.
KOMPOTTE: Cooked fruits, fresh or dried.
NACHSPEISEN: Desserts, sweet dishes.
NACHTISCH: Same as above.
SÜSS-SPEISEN: Desserts, sweet dishes.
KÄSE: Various cheeses offered.

A sumptuous array of superb pastries and desserts of all kinds will be displayed in every KONDITOREI (confectioner's or pastry shop) in Germany. It is here at the coffee hour in the later afternoon that most Germans prefer to enjoy their delectable desserts. The Konditorei, in addition to being the source of the sweets, also serves as a cafe with a series of small tables to accommodate its customers.

Desserts listed on menus to be eaten following a meal usually are fruit compotes or dishes of ice cream, often topped with whipped cream or served with fruit. Also, when in season, many fresh fruits, especially berries, are served with whipped cream, ice cream or Kirschwasser (a cherry brandy), or they are combined in a mixed fresh fruit salad.

Because so many German desserts are served with plain cream (SAHNE or RAHM), although these words may also mean whipped cream depending upon the dessert, or with whipped cream (SCHLAGRAHM or SCHLAGSAHNE), or ice cream (EIS, EISCREME or EISKREM), or with a pure white cherry brandy (KIRSCHWASSER), these preparations will not be repeated under the different desserts which they accompany.

ANANAS: Pineapple.
APFEL: Apple.
APFELMUS: Applesauce.
APFELRINGE: Apple rings.
APFELSTRUDEL: A sheet of thin dough with apple filling, rolled up and baked.
APFELSINEN: Oranges.
APRIKOSEN: Apricots.

81

ARME RITTER: Means "Poor Knights", and is a type of French toast–white bread soaked in egg batter, coated with breadcrumbs and fried. Served with sauteed apples or other fruit.

ART des HAUSES: Homemade, or made in the restaurant.

AUFLAUF: Soufflé, though it is more like a pudding, often made with eggs and rice, tapioca, bread, and baked in the oven.

BACKPFLAUME: Prune.

BANANE: Banana.

BAUMSTAMMEIS: Ice cream roll dessert.

BECHER: Goblet (dessert dish).

BEIGNETS: Fritters.

BERLINER PFANNKUCHEN: A round jam-filled doughnut without the hole, sprinkled with sugar.

BIRNE(N): Pear.

BIRNE "HELENE" or "SCHÖNE HELENE": A pear poached in syrup and served with vanilla ice cream and chocolate sauce.

BORKENSCHOKOLADE: Melted chocolate spread very thinly on a cookie sheet and cooled, then cut into squares and used to top desserts.

BRATAPFEL: Baked apple.

BROMBEEREN: Blackberries.

CANTALOUP: Cantaloupe.

CREME: Custard or cream filling.

CREME CARAMEL: Caramel custard.

CREMESPEISE: Custard.

CREPES SUCHARD: Thin dessert pancakes spread with chocolate sauce, chopped almonds, rolled, and sugar sprinkled on.

CREPES SUZETTE: Thin dessert pancakes filled with orange-flavored butter cream, usually flamed.

DATTELN: Date.

EIERSCHAUM: Beaten egg yolks and sugar cooked together, and then flavored with sweet wine.

EIS, EISCREME, EISKREM: Ice cream.

EISBECHER: Ice cream in a goblet or dessert dish, with or without fruit, liquor, whipped cream.

EISBOMBE: A molded frozen dessert.

EISTORTE: An ice cream cake either round or square. Ice cream can be mixed with fruit and spread on a base of some type of cookies often soaked in liquor, and can be topped with meringue and candied fruits.

ENGLISCHER KUCHEN: Loaf cake.

ERDBEEREN: Strawberries.

ERDBEEREN "ROMANOW": Strawberries mixed with port wine or with a liqueur, put into parfait glass, and topped with whipped cream.

ERDBEERCREME: Cream custard strawberry dessert.

ERDNUSS: Peanut.

FEIGEN: Figs.

FEINGEBÄCK: Fine or delicate pastry, cookies, wafers—baked goods.

FLAMBIERT(E): Flambeed.

FLÜSSIGE SAHNE: Thick cream, not whipped.

FRISCHE: Fresh.

FRÜCHTE(N): Fruit.

FRÜCHTECREME: Fruit custard.

FRUCHTEIS: Ice cream made with fruit in it.

FRÜCHTEBECHER: Ice cream with fruit, cream or Kirschwasser.

FRÜCHTE NACH JAHRESZEIT: Fruit in season.

FRUCHTSALAT: Fruit salad.

FRUCHTKALTSCHALE: A cold soup with white wine base and various types of pureed and sweetened fruits.

FÜRST-PÜCKLER-EIS: "Prince Puckler" ice cream—a slice of chocolate, vanilla and strawberry brick ice cream topped with whipped cream and fresh strawberries.

GARNIERT: Garnished.

GEBÄCK: Cookies, pastries, wafers—baked goods.

GEBACKENE: Baked.

GEFÜLLT: Filled.

GEFRORENES: A general term for various types of ice cream.

GEEISTER: Iced or chilled.

GEHOBELTEN: Shredded.

GEMISCHTES: Mixed or varied.

GEZUCKERT: Sugared.

GRAPEFRUIT: Grapefruit.

GRÜTZE: A pudding made with cooked fruit, usually berries.

HALBGEFRORENES: A molded frozen whipped cream or ice cream dessert.

HASELNUSS: Hazelnut.

HASELNUSS-RAHMBOMBE: A hazelnut cream, frozen, molded dessert.

HEISSEN: Hot or warm.

HIMBEEREN: Raspberries.

HONIGMELONE: Honey melon.

JOHANNISBEEREN: Red currant.

JOGHURT: Yogurt.

KAISERSCHMARREN mit KOMPOTT: A flat, unrolled omelette pancake made of flour, eggs and milk with raisins added to the batter. It is sprinkled with sugar and served with applesauce or stewed fruit.

KAFFEE: Coffee, or coffee-flavored.

KARAMEL-CREME: Caramel custard.

KÄSETORTE: Cheesecake.

KASTANIEN: Chestnuts.

KIRSCHEN: Cherries.

KIRSCHWASSER: A pure white cherry brandy.

KLEINE: Small.

KOMPOTT(E): Compote—whole fruit cooked in syrup; stewed fruit.

KÖNIGSKUCHEN: King's Cake—a rum-flavored loaf cake with almonds, raisins, currants.

KRONSBEEREN: A type of cranberry.

KRAPFEN: Fritters.

KREM: Custard or cream filling.

KUCHEN: Cake, tart or pastry.

KÜCHERL: Austrian word for fritters.

LIMONE: Lime.

MANDARINE: Tangerine.

MANDELN: Almonds.

MANDELCREME: Almond cream custard dessert.

MARASCHINO: A wild cherry liqueur.

MARMELADE: Jam.

MELONEN: Melons.

MERINGE: Meringue.

MIRABELLEN: Small yellow plums.

MOCCA: Coffee.

MOHRENKOPF: ''Moor's Head''—A dome-shaped individual white cake filled with custard or whipped cream and covered with hardened chocolate.

NACHSPEISEN or NACHTISCH: Dessert.

NACH WAHL: Of your choice.

NATUR: Plain.

NOUGAT: Almond and chocolate paste.

NOUGAT EISTORTE: An ice cream cake made with an almond and chocolate paste.

OBST: Fruit.

OBSTKUCHEN: Fruit tart or pastry.

OBSTSALAT: Fruit salad.

OMELETTE: Omelette with sweet filling.

OMELETTE mit KONFITÜRE: Omelette filled with jam.

OMELETTE SOUFFLE: This is really a soufflé in which egg yolks and egg whites are beaten separately with sugar and flavorings, then combined and baked in the oven.

ORANGEN: Oranges.

PALATSCHINKEN: Austrian for sweet jam-filled pancakes.

PAMPELMUSE: Grapefruit.

PARFAIT: Alternating layers of ice cream, fruit, or syrup and whipped cream served in a tall narrow stem glass.

PFANNKUCHEN: Pancake.

PFIRSICH(EN): Peach.

PFIRSICH "CARDINAL": Peach poached in syrup, served with ice cream and a puree of strawberries with slivered almonds on top.

PFIRSICH "MELBA": Half a fresh peach poached in syrup, filled with a scoop of vanilla ice cream and topped with fresh crushed and sweetened raspberries.

PFLAUMEN: Plums.

PREISELBEEREN: Cranberries.

PRINZREGENTENTORTE: Prince Regent Cake–a rich multi-layed cake, each layer spread with a cooked chocolate butter-cream frosting, then the cake is covered with hardened melted chocolate or other such icing.

PUDDING: Pudding.

RAHM: Cream, plain or whipped.

REICHE AUSWAHL: Full assortment.

ROSINEN: Raisins.

RHABARBER: Rhubarb.

RINGE: Rings or slices, as of apples.

ROTE GRÜTZE: A type of fruit pudding–various types of berries which are cooked, strained, sweetened, then mixed with some starch to make a thick mixture which is put into molds and served cold either with cream or a sauce.

RUM: Rum.

SAFT: Juice.

SAHNE: Cream, plain or whipped.

SAHNEHALBGEFRORENES: A molded frozen whipped cream dessert.

SALZBURGER NOCKERLN: An Austrian dessert of a sweet dough which is shaped into dumplings, poached in milk and served with hot vanilla sauce.

SANDDORN: A flavoring made from a small berry which has high vitamin content.

SAUCE: Sauce.

SAUERKIRSCHEN: Sour cherries.

SCHATTENMORELLEN: Dark red sour cherries.

SCHAUMSPEISE: A mousse, a frozen molded dessert often with whipped cream and a gelatin base.

SCHEIBEN: Slice.

SCHLAGRAHM: Whipped cream.

SCHLAGSAHNE: Whipped cream.

SCHLOTFEGER mit SAHNE: A long tube of pastry filled with whipped cream and covered with chocolate.

SCHNEE: Beaten egg whites, sweetened when served with, or as a dessert.

SCHOKOLADEN: Chocolate.

SCHNITTE: Slice or portion.

SCHOKOLADENCREMETORTE: A chocolate cream layer cake filled with a rich chocolate cream mixture.

SCHWARZE JOHANNISBEEREN: Black currant.

SCHWEIZER REIS: A molded rice dessert served with a sauce.

SCHWEIZER SAHNEREIS: A molded cream rice pudding.

SORBET: Sherbet, the French word for it.

SOSSE: Sauce.

STACHELBEEREN: Gooseberries.

STREUSELKUCHEN: Made of yeast dough. It is a type of coffeecake with a topping of crumbled butter, sugar and flour flavored with cinnamon.

STÜCK: Piece or portion.

TAGES-DESSERT or -SÜSS-SPEISEN: Dessert of the day.

TEEBLATT: An oval pastry like a napoleon without filling, and with sugar sprinkled on top.

TEEGEBÄCK: Tea cakes or petit fours.

TOPFENSTRUDEL: Strudel dough is spread with a creamed cottage cheese mixture containing eggs, sugar and vanilla; then rolled and baked.

TÖRTCHEN: Tarts.

TORTE(N): Cake, especially layer cake, also open-faced pie or pastry made in large round flat form, with custard or cream filling, fruit, nuts, and topped with perhaps whipped cream or a cooked cream frosting.

TRAUBEN: Grapes.

TRAUBENZUCKER: Grape sugar.

TUNKE: Sauce.

VANILLE: Vanilla.

VOM BRETT: From the tray or cart–a variety of cakes and pastries from which you make your choice.

PRICES ARE NOT ACTUAL ONES

ARTE

nung und Mehrwertsteuer

. . . .	DM 5,50
. . . .	DM 7,00
. . . .	DM 7,80
. . . .	DM 11,20
alat	DM 9,60
offelpüree	DM 8,40
udeln	DM 9,80
kartoffeln	DM 9,80
salat	DM 11,00
. . . .	DM 11,20
üree	DM 11,80
eisrand, Salat	DM 12,00
Salatteller	DM 13,00
hkkartoffeln	DM 13,40
gurke	DM 13,40
rtoffeln	DM 13,60
, Pommes frites	DM 13,80
eller	DM 13,80
e Erbsen	DM 13,80
Butterreis	DM 14,80
Butternudeln	DM 15,00
. . . .	DM 17,00
eis, Salat	DM 18,50
mmes frites	DM 19,00
eller	DM 19,00
. . . .	DM 19,50
rtoffeln	DM 19,50
nes frites	DM 21,00